THE INVESTOR'S

MUTUAL FUNDS EXPLAINED

THE BASICS AND BEYOND

ROBERT C. UPTON, JR.

PROBUS PUBLISHING COMPANY
Chicago, Illinois

Authorization to photocopy items for internal or personal use, or the internal or personal use of specific clients, is granted by PROBUS PUBLISHING COMPANY, provided that the U.S. $7.00 per page fee is paid directly to Copyright Clearance Center, 27 Congress Street, Salem, MA 01970, USA; Phone: 1-508-744-3350. For those organizations that have been granted a photocopy license by CCC, a separate system of payment has been arranged. The fee code for users of the Transactional Reporting Service is 1-55738-211-5/91/$00.00 + $7.00.

Library of Congress Cataloging-in-Publication Data

Upton, Robert C.
   Mutual funds explained : the basics and beyond / Robert C. Upton.
      p.   cm. — (Investor's quick reference)
   Includes bibliographical references and index.
   ISBN 1-55738-211-5 : $12.95
   1. Mutual funds. I. Title. II. Series.
HG4530.U68   1992
332.63'27—dc 20   91-30365
                                                                        CIP

ISBN 1-55738-211-5

Printed in the United States of America

IPC

   2   3   4   5   6   7   8   9   0

CONTENTS

PREFACE

There's a sucker born every minute.
—*Phineas Taylor Barnum*

P. T. Barnum's "sucker" is one who ventures uninformed into the world of the professional, convinced that success is possible without understanding fundamentals. Shortcuts and predigested advice nourish the investing "sucker." Would you risk the hazards of scuba diving without knowing your equipment? Or attempt to pilot an airplane without understanding the instruments? How long would a football player who couldn't execute a block or make a basic tackle survive the NFL? Vince Lombardi, aside from inspiring his players, coached "basic football." His philosophy was that basic principles, intelligently and confidently applied, yield success.

The reading public is swamped with "how-to" books. This book is not another. You find no "hot tips" or surefire financial formulas here. There are none.

This book does not attempt a comprehensive coverage of investments. The spectrum is too exhaustive for one volume. The focus of this book is on mutual funds—more specifically, the understanding of goals, income, and growth and their relation to your selection of a mutual fund. This book is a product of almost 25 years of my professional investing. It is taken from my syndicated financial column, college classroom lectures, and questions most frequently asked by my readers, students, and clients. With an understanding of the basics of mutual fund selection, you will be not only prepared but also confident about venturing into this rewarding field of investing.

I am sometimes asked why I do not recommend specific mutual funds in my weekly column or in this book. Dr. John Ritchie, Jr., professor of finance at Temple University in Philadelphia, Pennsylvania, and professional editor of this book, wanted to know. "Why don't you name the example funds?" asked Dr. Ritchie. "Wouldn't the reader be more comfortable being able to check your statistics?" These are legitimate concerns, voiced by an educator and economist.

To begin, my purpose is not to recommend specific mutual funds. The mutual fund examples are illustrations of principles. Focus on the principle, rather than the example. Particular care was taken to select examples that do not suggest unrealistic performance. In most cases several similar funds of like objective and longevity could serve equally well as examples. Ideally you will look at several different mutual funds and weigh them against the suggested standards before you invest. Each fund has slightly different performance, of course, but long-term results are often similar. Performance figures change; the principles of investing are more stable.

Particular care is taken to offer you the opportunity to focus on the theory of investing without the annoyance of being silently sold the author's pet mutual funds. This allows you the benefit of independently weighing your mutual fund selections against the suggested criteria. Editors and readers generally prefer objectivity.

A mutual fund must fit you. It must answer your long-range goals, satisfy your risk tolerance, and in general make you comfortable owning it.

The examples are real. They are historical examples of how a variety of mutual funds can meet specific needs.

The examples are not intended to excite you over a particular fund but rather to illustrate a point. There can be no assurance that any fund will meet future objectives. Performance is only a report card on past management. Investment return and principal value of fund shares fluctuate, so shares of any fund may be worth more or less in the future.

The final reason mutual funds are not identified by name is to prevent mistaking an example for a recommendation. A mutual fund's prospectus discusses the fund's financial objective, management philosophy, risks, costs, and much more. Every fund must have a prospectus, and no fund can be recommended without offering a prospectus. After reading this book you should think of the prospectus as a prerequisite to investing. When a specific mutual fund is discussed, its prospectus must accompany it. This rigid regulation is for your protection, and you are reminded of it throughout the book.

The illustrations and examples used in this book are similar to those used in my weekly column. No mutual fund is ever identified by name or fund group. The principles of mutual fund investing developed in this book can be worth more to your financial success than any list of past winners. As you read this book, the proper process of selecting a mutual fund will become apparent. Chapter 1 sets direction. What do you want your mutual fund to accomplish? You are encouraged to be specific. Set goals, risk tolerance, and length of time your money is to be deposited, to name only a few considerations.

After your goals and objectives are clear, look for the right manager for your money. In Chapter 2 we see how mutual funds are professionally managed and how to measure the effectiveness of your money manager.

Chapter 3 unravels the mystery of different funds. Mutual funds pursue different purposes and carry different risks. Here you fit your objectives into one or more of six general categories of mutual funds.

Chapters 4 and 5 narrow your selection process even more. From general categories of mutual funds, you are introduced to funds for specific purposes. Time, compounding, and dollar cost averaging all play an important role in your financial plan. You see examples of how they work for you.

By this time you are on the way to selecting your mutual fund. Chapters 6 and 7 now introduce you to mutual fund numbers that make sense. Here you learn how to evaluate your fund by understanding your statements.

Mutual fund quotations in the newspaper are no longer a mystery. You learn where to look for the cost of buying and managing your mutual fund. None are free. You become comfortable reading a prospectus and learn to think of it as your investing partner, there to answer your questions.

Chapter 8 is good news and bad news. The bad news is that mutual funds do lose value in an unfriendly stock market. The good news is that carefully selected mutual funds have a way of recovering.

Finally, there is a wrap-up of 10 easy rules to serve as your checklist before investing in a mutual fund you plan to buy, or for evaluating the mutual fund you already own.

Mutual fund investing is exciting. I hope to share that excitement with you.

Robert Upton

CHAPTER 1

GOALS AND OBJECTIVES: OR, WHERE AM I GOING AND HOW DO I GET THERE?

> Shallow men believe in luck, wise
> and strong men in cause and effect.
> —*Ralph Waldo Emerson*

I had a college buddy who wore brown wing tip shoes. He said they felt so good he couldn't understand why everybody didn't wear brown wing tip shoes. I admit it would solve a lot of problems. Walk into any shoe store...

"Good day, may I help you?"

"Yes, I'd like something in a brown wing tip, like the pair in the window...right there...no, not that pair, the one next to them...that's it!"

"An excellent choice. Let me see if I have that little number in your size."

See how simple it would be if everyone wore brown wing tip shoes? But they don't.

So storekeepers must stock hundreds of different shoes in assorted colors and styles, so you have the opportunity to squeeze your petite size nine into a size six pump...because it's *your* "thing."

I once knew a stockbroker who put everyone into brown wing tip shoes. To him, everybody was there to gamble, and he was there to take bets! Anyone holding a stock more than a week was either a long-term investor or had inadvertently been overlooked in a frenzied effort to liquidate his "bigger clients." In his mind, every "client" had the same objective: make Mr. Quick-Turn commissions!

I hope you never allow anyone to identify this as your objective. Your investing program is a very personal thing. It requires in-depth planning and periodic review. As needs and circumstances change, so does your investment plan.

I believe so strongly in the need for clearly defined objectives and a workable plan to meet those objectives that I have devoted numerous columns to this subject. Since mutual funds are designed for different purposes, let's begin by answering a few questions...

Why Isn't One Investment Plan Right for Everyone?

Before investing, decide what you want your investments to do. Investing is simply using money to make more money. Investment dollars are dedicated funds not used for daily living essentials.

You might choose to invest in mortgages, real estate, life insurance, or securities (stocks and bonds). They're all different, and no single investment fits the needs of every person.

Since most mutual funds limit their investments to securities, let's focus on some of the reasons you might want to own a mutual fund. Many prefer mutual funds because they are easily bought and sold. They represent variety and flexibility of interests, as well as absentee ownership or creditorship. Mutual funds can be bought at varying prices, from very low to very high, and small sums of money can be invested at convenient intervals. Mutual funds can be selected, often with excellent results, by persons having limited investment backgrounds.

When investing in a mutual fund, you can profit in two ways. First, you may receive dividends, which in theory are paid to compensate you for the use of your money. Since the market value of mutual funds fluctuates, you also may profit when selling your mutual fund shares if they have increased in value.

The other side of the coin, however, is that fluctuation also means the value of your shares can depreciate. If it is necessary that you sell shares at a depressed price, you could lose part of your original investment. That is why it is recommended that investing in mutual funds be considered a long-term investment program. Don't gamble on short-term market performance and be forced to sell your shares when the price is down.

Regardless of what mutual fund you select, it should meet your goals. A basic rule of investing is that it should not be done on impulse. Know what you want before you buy. Then determine if your selection will do that. In short, does it meet your needs?

For example, if you buy a mutual fund for income, then expect that fund to provide enough dividends (stock or equity mutual funds provide dividends) to meet your needs. In addition, be reasonably sure that this income will be paid regularly and on time.

Whether or not you get your income depends on the ability of that mutual fund to generate income. It's generally true that the higher the income, the greater the risk. A U.S. government-guaranteed bond fund may not provide as much income as a portfolio of unsecured notes managed by another mutual fund. On the other hand, the obligation of the government to pay interest can offer peace of mind. So if you're aiming for maximum income, chances are you'll have to sacrifice some safety. To put it another way, there's no such thing as a free lunch.

If income is secondary, however, and you're after capital appreciation, you may consider a mutual fund investing in securities you think have a strong potential for gain. But remember, this mutual fund probably offers more market risk.[1]

One thing you can be certain of is that no mutual fund can simultaneously offer you minimum risk, attractive income, and outstanding growth potential. If a mutual fund features one of these, the others will be secondary or practically nonexistent. At certain times, however, it may be possible to select a mutual fund which potentially offers some modest combination of these features over a period of time. We'll talk about these later.

What's My Personality Got to Do with Investing?

In determining investment goals—safety, income, or growth—first consider your personality and temperament. Are you self-assured, comfortable in making decisions, or are you prone to be swayed by the opinion of others?

Someone who owns and operates a business, regardless of size, is usually more comfortable in making an investment decision than a housewife whose major activities are confined to the management of her home. (Please, ladies, excuse this example!) A competitive business environment makes investment decisions necessary—how much inventory to hold, where and when to issue credit, and so on. So making investment decisions, weighing risk against reward, and applying such decisions to a business situation are part of management.

On the other hand, there are those who jump at the first suggestion of another, even though that person may not be as successful as they. Try to explain it? It's just human nature. Remember the old story of two people looking at a partially filled glass of water—one sees it half-full; the other, half-empty. The optimist sees a slight drop in the market value of a mutual fund as a normal correction, to be followed by a traditional move forward—another buying opportunity. The pessimist sees the drop in price as the first step toward a total loss. If you're a pessimist, you might be uncomfortable with an aggressive growth fund that makes radical moves up and down. You would probably be more comfortable in something less risky.

The time you have to devote to investments is also important. Investment situations are constantly changing. You must be aware of these changes and be ready and willing to react. If your time is limited and your investments lie unattended for long periods, mutual funds may be the answer.

You see the necessity of considering your own personality before beginning an investment program or selecting a mutual fund.

What about People Who Are Retired or Have a Family?

Age is a strong consideration in your investment decisions. Notice how conservatism comes with age. You may think of it as wisdom. Wisdom, or has your position in life changed?

With age comes the awareness that a serious investment error could jeopardize the security that has taken years to accumulate. The closer to retirement, the fewer the years to rebuild. So a more conservative attitude is often taken. Now preserving capital becomes more important.

Young folks often say, "Shoot the works." Win or lose, there are years ahead to rebuild. This attitude can be defended, although not necessarily recommended for everyone. Our free enterprise economy needs those willing to take calculated risks. Without this pioneering spirit, implementation of advanced ideas would never materialize. Investment risk, however, is quite different from gambling. Weighing risk based on fact is investing. Taking chances based on odds is gambling. The point is, age is an important factor in deciding risk. And with age generally comes conservatism.

Another strong consideration is responsibilities. A young person beginning a career with the additional responsibility of one or more children must weigh these responsibilities. The most protection for the fewest dollars should supersede any forced savings that would reduce family protection.

Many insurance contracts today offer minimum protection for maximum dollars. Your monthly premium is divided between paying the insurer for your life protection and depositing the rest into *cash value*. This can result in too few dollars going to protect your family. Insurance companies call it *forced savings*. Before you are "forced" into saving, make certain your family is adequately protected in the event of your untimely death. Investigate the pure protection of term insurance before you commit to any savings or investment program. It's wise to have funds accessible without penalty or loss, for emergency use.

Financial needs change. How they are met should depend on your responsibilities.

Why Should I Start Investing Today?

Today's decisions should consider tomorrow's needs. There's a direct relationship between the amount of money you need to accumulate and the number of years you have to do it.

For example, if you plan to build a $12,000 education fund, have 20 years to do it, and expect an annual rate of return of 12 percent, you have to invest only a little over $12 each month. Wait 5 years, and with 15 years left you'll need over $24 each month. Procrastinate another 10 years, and it'll take almost $147 every month to have that same $12,000 at college time.

Time can be a real asset when planning for a child's education or for your retirement. The more time you have, the fewer dollars you need now. Don't let time slip away.

What about Investment Advisers?

Investment advice is only as good as the source. I'm reminded of a cartoon showing two hoboes sitting on a park bench sharing investment strategy. I generally discount advice from ne'er-do-wells or those who stand to benefit from their advice.

Sound investing is not based on hot tips or hunches. Before you select a broker or adviser, first meet with him and learn his philosophy on investing. Get to know that person. Once you choose a broker, take him into your confidence. Explain your goals and financial resources. The more that person knows you and your needs, the better he will be able to serve you. It's your money. Ask questions and get answers! Don't be shy!

Financial security is important. Doesn't it make sense to be as selective in accepting advice on your investments as you are with other important decisions? Yet so many are sold an investment without understanding it or any risks it presents.

Your financial adviser should meet certain requirements. First, you should be reasonably assured that he is honest and will work in your best interest. He should make every effort to determine what *you* want your investments to do, not sell you a bill of goods based on what *he* wants them to do. What are his credentials? Any professional is delighted to discuss educational background, graduate study, specialized training, and registration. Ask for references. Investigate your financial adviser as you would investigate your physician or attorney. It'll be time well spent.

Once you've established confidence, be candid, but demand that the information you give is held in absolute confidence.

What Are the Three Rules of Investing?

There is no simple formula for successful investing. If there were it would include three basic elements: (1) understand what you buy, (2) buy value at a reasonable price, and (3) be patient.

Understanding your investment is so basic, it's often neglected. Too often an investment is made with no ideas of what it is. We've all chuckled at the remark, "Don't confuse me with facts." But facts—or more accurately, how they are presented—may confuse even a seasoned investor and totally mystify a beginner. This shouldn't be. It's vital to understand your investment—the good and the bad, the risks and the rewards. If the investment is unduly complicated, ask questions until you're satisfied with the answers. Fully understand the objective of any investment. Is that your objective? The more you understand, the more comfortable you will be with your investments. If you're not comfortable with an investment you own, that's a good indication you shouldn't own it. Ask questions and get answers.

I recently had the opportunity to visit with a group of professional money managers responsible for more than $9 billion worth of investment assets. Their prudent search for value is documented by more than 50 years of consistently superior results. Of course, they boast of no magic formula; it's dedicated research by a team of knowledgeable professionals that makes them successful. However, when asked to sum up their combined philosophies, they agreed their success depends on recognizing and buying value at reasonable prices.

Value buying demands both research and discipline. A stock may be judged undervalued for various reasons. For example, if an industry is out of favor, the market value of the stocks within that industry might go lower and become even better values. If this is the case and the fundamentals are still positive, it's an opportunity for the value investor to buy selectively.

Patience is a vital ingredient of value investing. Generally the key to buying value is to recognize it early. It could take several years for the value of your investment to materialize. This waiting period demands both patience and confidence. The most successful investors know it takes time for their investment to double, triple, or more.

Although there is no magic time period, professional managers generally agree that five years is reasonable. This allows for the normal fluctuations of the stock market, for adjustments in the economy, and for the value of your investment to mature and be recognized in the marketplace. In five years your original investment could double at a reasonable 15 percent annual compounding.

With investing there are few guarantees, but understanding your investments, seeking value, and waiting for them to develop will generally put you ahead in the race for financial security.

Endnote

[1] Market risk is that part of a security's risk that is common to all securities of the same general class. This is a risk that cannot be eliminated by diversification. Since mutual funds invest in stocks and bonds, they are subject to market risk.

Chapter 2

CHOOSING A PROFESSIONAL MONEY MANAGER: OR, WHY CAN'T I DO IT MYSELF WHEN I BALANCE MY CHECKBOOK?

> Put not your trust in money
> but put your money in trust.
> —*Oliver Wendell Holmes*

Some years ago, Frank Sinatra sang "I Did It My Way." The title tells the story. There are a lot of people who like to "do it their way"—particularly when it comes to investing. Right or wrong, they want to be captain of their ship.

But not everyone can or likes to be the captain. Being a passenger has advantages. It's usually more comfortable and certainly less time-consuming.

When your investments are managed by someone else, you sit back and either reap the harvest or suffer the loss. Bank savings and life insurance are the best-known types of managed investments outside the securities area. Usually these have some guarantee of principal and income. Since there are guarantees, the income is usually low. This is understandable, since the bank or life insurance company must project how much their investments will earn after operation costs. Only then can they decide how much to safely and reasonably guarantee and still show a profit for their shareholders. These investments don't require a considerable amount of management research, since you're guaranteed a fixed income regardless of how well management does.

It's a lazy way to invest. There's not much risk, but there's also not much reward. It might even leave you with a warm feeling that your money is "working," but it's not working too hard.

Where does that leave you if you want your money not only to produce a reasonable income now but also to grow over the years? The answer is a professional money manager—someone who, for a reasonable fee, will manage your money and pass on the income and growth. Of course, the key is consistency. Remember, the manager gets paid regardless of the profits you make. So make sure he earns his keep. With mutual fund managers there is a wealth of information to measure their performance against other managers, market indexes, and the economy in general. So...

How Can I Get Professional Money Management?

What options are there if you lack experience, time, or courage to personally manage investments, or if you believe others can get better results? There are several ways to enjoy professional management—closed-end investment company shares, discretionary accounts with brokers, registered investment advisers, special trusts, sales and timing via subscription services, newsletters, financial publications, and mutual funds. Let's talk about mutual funds. A reasonable question is...

How Many Folks Use Mutual Funds?

For more than 50 years, mutual funds have offered a convenient way for individuals to invest. But during the 1980s, their growth mushroomed.

Figures released recently by the Investment Company Institute (ICI) reveal that "one in four households today invests in the nearly 3,000 mutual funds." This is impressive, considering that less than 6 percent of households invested in mutual funds 10 years ago (Figure 2-1).

By the end of the 1980s, Americans had increased the assets they hold in mutual funds from $94.5 billion to just under $1 trillion (Figure 2-2). Several basic trends contributed to this phenomenal growth.

Money market funds exploded during the early 1980s. For the first time, many people invested in funds because of the attractive yields available during a period of double-digit inflation.

Once inflation subsided in 1982, investors turned to income-oriented funds.[1] According to the ICI, assets of bond funds increased 18-fold during the decade, compared to the 10-fold increase in all mutual funds.

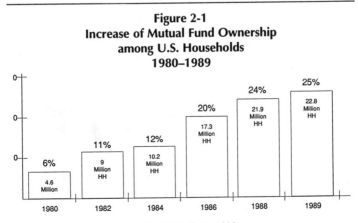

Figure 2-1
Increase of Mutual Fund Ownership
among U.S. Households
1980–1989

Source: Investment Company Institute, Sept. 1989

Figure 2-2
Assets of Mutual Funds
(billions of dollars)

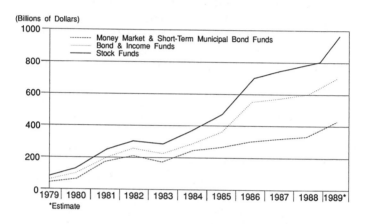

Source: Investment Company Institute, Dec. 1989

Assets in tax-exempt municipal bond funds also rose in the 1980s, from $39.4 billion in 1985 to more than $102 billion in 1989. In addition, government bond funds and Government National Mortgage Association funds grew from less than 1 percent of all mutual fund assets in 1980 to more than 11 percent in 1989.

A combination of factors during the 1980s enhanced the popularity of not only income funds but all mutual funds:

- the opportunity for Americans to establish Individual Retirement Accounts (IRAs)

- a prolonged bull market

- the expansion of fund types—precious metals funds, sector funds, international and global funds, to name a few

All these factors led to mutual fund shareholder accounts doubling between 1985 and 1987. In fact, the ICI says that monthly sales in 1985 and 1986 routinely exceeded annual sales for any complete year prior to 1980.

In 1987 the bull market was disrupted. The bond market suffered several declines, followed by the stock market crash in October.

This disturbance, however, was only temporary. In 1988 and 1989 mutual fund sales and assets soared to new heights. In 1989 people invested nearly $120 billion in stock and bond mutual funds, making it the third-highest year ever in terms of sales (Figure 2-3).

What's ahead for mutual funds? Institute president David Silver says that with the American population

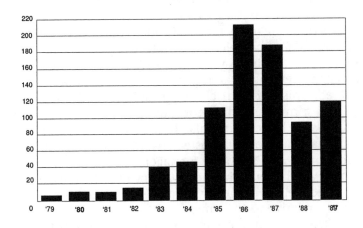

Figure 2-3
Total Sales of Stock & bond Funds*
(billions of dollars)

* Incluses reinvested dividends
** Estimate

Source: Investment Company Institute, Dec. 1989

growing older and needing more money for retirement, the cost of a college education continuing to rise faster than inflation, and individual investors' increased wariness of volatile securities markets, "It is reasonable to assume that pooled investments, such as mutual funds, will become even more important to investors in the years ahead."

These are, of course, all interesting numbers and opinions, but...

What Can a Mutual Fund Do for Me?

The most fundamental fact about any mutual fund is that it is simply a method of managing money. Once you invest, your money is pooled with that of other investors and managed under the terms of the fund's prospectus. How well you do depends on how well you select a manager.

There are no guarantees, but generally a successful method used over an extended period of changing economic conditions is a good guide to choosing a manager. Today there are many mutual fund managers to consider.

Look, for example, at one of the oldest mutual funds in America. This 65-year-old fund has weathered two stock market crashes, a depression, three major wars, and the administration of eleven presidents and has never missed a quarterly dividend payment. That in itself is impressive, but consider also that during this time many national and global "disasters" would have discouraged most investors. Yet these managers continued to invest whenever they had the money. They used their expertise to selectively manage investments between stocks and bonds, relative to the times.

The year they began, the Harding administration was riddled with scandal. Had you entrusted $10,000 to them, in that year, 1924, then by 1930, the year after the stock market crash, it would have been worth $15,762.

The depression years were difficult. More than 12 million Americans were jobless—definitely not a friendly investment climate. But by 1935 your investment was worth $16,498.

In 1938 war clouds began to gather. In the following years, Hitler invaded Poland; France fell; Pearl Harbor was attacked; and we were at war. That year your investment fell to $14,336.

With war came rationing, price controls, and a full wartime economy. When war ended in 1945, economists predicted a full recession; hardly a time to invest, considering your nest egg was at an all-time high of $32,473.

During the next 10 years, a lot happened. The Dow Jones Industrial Average topped 200 and was "too high." The cold war began. There was the Berlin blockade, Korean "police action," an excess profits tax, and the governmental takeover of the steel mills. In 1954 the Dow was certainly too high at 300, and your original $10,000 was worth $103,317.

The next 10 years were critical world times. There was a crisis in the Suez, and a recession at home. Cuba fell to Castro, and a Berlin Wall was erected. When John F. Kennedy was assassinated in 1963, your investment was worth $265,406.

When world problems seemed to relax, national unrest erupted. Civil rights issues exploded, and riots plagued U.S. cities. Martin Luther King was assassinated, and the war in Vietnam continued to escalate. There was tight money and a falling market. When business activity declined, wage and price freezes were initiated. Trade deficits, oil prices, Watergate, New York City's financial crisis were all news in the early 1970s.

The rest of the decade was highlighted by an economic recovery that stalled, a U.S. dollar that dropped, and inflation like we had never seen. In spite of this, by 1980 your investment was worth $779,387.

Although inflation and high interest dominated the first two years of the 1980s, by 1983 a bull market began to heat up. Budget and trade deficits plus a host of other old problems erupted, but the bull roared on until October 19, 1987, when it stumbled. The prophets of economic doom were again out in force, but when 1987 ended your investment was worth $1,712,589.

Sixty-five years is not an overly impressive time in the overall course of history. However, during that time a tremendous amount happened in this country. Legendary, larger-than-life personalities influenced the way we live—Charles Lindbergh, Red Grange, Babe Ruth, Clarence Darrow, Louis Armstrong, Amelia Earhart, F. Scott Fitzgerald, Jack Dempsey, George Gershwin, Ernest Hemingway, William Faulkner, Al Jolson, and others. And mutual funds influenced the way we invest. Today, with more than 3,000 mutual funds and assets over $1 trillion, the mutual fund industry is one of the largest sources of investment dollars for America's corporations and offers the markets a major means of liquidity.

That's an impressive record for an industry whose first fund began in Boston in 1924.

In a mutual fund a group of investors pool their money and own shares of an investment trust. The money is professionally managed, the results are reported in a uniform manner to all shareholders, and the securities are held by a custodian bank. Technically, a mutual fund, or open-end investment company, is a corporation without fixed-equity capitalization that consistently sells and redeems its shares.

Sound complicated? It's not. It simply means the mutual fund doesn't have a specific number of shares to offer, as does a normal corporation. The fund always stands ready to sell additional shares or to redeem outstanding ones—hence the term *open-end*.

What's the value of these shares? A fund's value is quoted daily in the financial section of most major newspapers. The *bid price* quoted is the net asset value (what all the securities in the portfolio added together are worth, divided by the number of shares in the fund). The *offered price* is the net asset value plus the maximum sales charge. We'll see more how the numbers work in Chapter 6.

What Exactly Is a Mutual Fund?

I read a mutual fund's annual report, which is the fund's accounting to shareholders for the past business year. In such a report, the fund's managers usually highlight the fund and compare their performance to the stock market's leading indicators—the Dow Jones Average of 30 Industrial Stocks or Standard & Poor's Composite Index.

I was impressed by the fund's numbers, but the most captivating feature was the real-life story of the grandparents who introduced their two grandchildren to investing. They gave life to nebulous terms like *mutual funds* and *stock*. Here's what happened when the children spent a day with their grandparents learning what investments in mutual funds were all about.

Grandma and Grandpa had just bought some shares in a mutual fund for the children. "What's a mutual fund?" asked the children. Grandpa explained that they were now part owners of many different businesses. Folks invest their money in the fund, and the fund buys stocks of companies that they think are good businesses. If the companies do well and their stock goes up, the fund shares are worth more. "Someday this could help put you through college," Grandma added.

Grandpa went on to tell the children how the value of the shares change almost every day, depending on how well their stocks do. He showed them how to find the price on the financial page under "Mutual Funds" in the daily newspaper. He circled their fund with a red pencil.

"What companies do we own, Grandpa?"

"One is the company that puts out this newspaper," he answered. Grandma picked up a box of cereal the children were sharing for breakfast. "And the company who makes this cereal," she said. "Also, the company who makes my refrigerator, oven, and coffee machine. You own a part of all these companies through your mutual fund."

As the day progressed, the children learned that the car Grandpa drove, the fuel that powered it, the fast-food franchise where they lunched, the clothes they wore, and the department store they visited were all part of companies they owned through their mutual fund. Grandma and Grandpa brought investments to life for the children. After all, if they liked the products enough to use them, didn't it make good sense to also invest in them? I liked this visit. It was real.

As I continued to page through the annual report, I came to the "Investment Portfolio." I read it. Familiar names took on new meaning through the products they offer. Autos, tires, utilities, paper, aircraft, electronics, appliances—four pages of companies who produce products and services that I use and that make my life more enjoyable. It made me proud to realize that I owned a small part of this.

But mutual funds manage billions of dollars. I like individual treatment, so...

Should I Have My Money Privately Managed?

There are two ways to have money professionally managed. One is private professional management, and the other is public professional management.

Through private management you entrust your money to an investment adviser or advisory service. Some accept accounts as small as $50,000, but generally the top firms only consider sums of $200,000 or more. Most major services don't accept smaller accounts. If, however, you want and qualify for private professional management, it's essential to conduct an in-depth study of the investment team you choose to manage your money.

To deposit money with strangers without a complete study of the firm's reputation, references, past performance, business longevity, and the like is the quickest way I know to permanently separate you from your money.

Some investors are mesmerized by the term *private investment* advice. Practically speaking, if the accounts average only $50,000 to $75,000 each, imagine how many accounts an adviser must manage to make his time profitable. Even with private management, once an investment position is decided, it's generally executed in all accounts sharing the same objectives. You may feel like you're getting special, individual treatment, but in fact you're part of the group. Of course, technically it's still individually managed.

So you wonder...

Should I Throw My Money Into a Pool?

If the amount you have to invest is less than $100,000, you might consider public professional management, using mutual funds.

The name *mutual funds* describes the investment. You are pooling your money with the money of others for your "mutual" benefit. You may have $1,000 to invest. By yourself you couldn't get much diversification. Neither could you have your investment privately managed. But if you find 1,000 other people wanting to invest together, you represent over a million dollars of investable funds. Now you're big enough to hire a professional money manager. Your manager is responsible to you for the performance of your investment. Your manager must uniformly report on its progress. This is public professional management.

You should choose your public money manager with the same care you would select a private money manager. An excellent reputation, competence, and consistency of performance should be absolute requirements. Does the management philosophy reflect your goals and objectives?

While you're thinking about this, ask yourself...

Is There a Yardstick to Measure Results?

It's easy to talk about good money management, but how do you find it? Standard & Poor's 500 Stock Index is a widely used yardstick to measure the stock market. It indicates the general direction of stocks and at what percent they are changing. But first...

What Is the Standard & Poor's Index?

Depending upon whom you ask, either the Dow Jones Industrial Average or Standard & Poor's 500 Composite Price Index (S&P 500) is the most dependable indicator of the overall performance of the stock market.

Because the S&P 500 monitors 500 select issues compared to the Dow's 30, however, it seems to be the favorite measurement for mutual funds. Not only do professional money managers use the S&P index to gauge their performance, there are even index funds designed to emulate its portfolio makeup in order to equal its performance.

The S&P 500 is not a fixed selection of stocks but undergoes continuous review and changes. Selecting the stocks to be added to the S&P 500 and deciding which ones will be eliminated is not a hit-and-miss system. A recent report by Albert S. Neubert of Standard & Poor's Corporation explained how the S&P Index Committee makes these important changes.

The committee consists of a select group of seven Standard & Poor's managers and executives. Their purpose is to set the overall policy and objectives of the S&P 500 and to establish guidelines and criteria for adding or dropping a company from the index. While attempting to keep a consistency in the composition of the index, the committee also tries to avoid excessive turnover.

One of the major reasons for change in the index is the condition of the economy. An example of this in recent years is the greater number of takeovers, mergers, and leveraged buyouts. Neubert explained that during the 1970s, one or two changes per year in the composition of the index was common, while during the last few years, as many as 25 to 30 changes per year have been required. Last year there were 27 changes. Neubert went on to say that because of a pattern of increased volume and market gains in a stock the day after inclusion in the S&P 500, "strict confidentiality is maintained."

A company may be removed from the index for a number of reasons. The most obvious and common is a merger or acquisition. In these cases the company is not removed until the committee is certain the stock will halt trading. Less-common causes are bankruptcy or a decrease in representatives. In these cases the committee allows events to become clearly defined before a vote for removal, which must then be a unanimous decision.

Monitoring S&P index changes is a simple and effective way to keep abreast of changing corporate and economic conditions. "Because response to economic change is the key to the S&P 500's respect among investors, the S&P 500 Index Committee constantly monitors emerging industries for possible inclusion in the Index," Neubert said. A review of the 500 not only finds the traditional leading industries but now reveals emerging groups like telecommunications equipment manufacturers, biotechnology and health care companies, high-tech electronics firms, and more.

Whether you are an individual stock investor or a mutual fund shareholder, you will find Standard & Poor's 500 Composite Price Index a reliable yardstick against which to measure your performance or that of your money manager.

It makes sense to use this index as a standard to measure how well professional money managers perform. For example, if the S&P for a specified period is up 10 percent and your mutual fund is up only 5 percent, your money manager is not doing as well as the market. On the other hand, if the portfolio's investments have gained more than the S&P, then it is outperforming the market. A money manager is paid to outperform the market when it's going up and protect you when it's coming down. The S&P index is the standard most often used to measure the effectiveness of money managers.

Recently the editors of a major weekly business magazine made a study of professional money managers. They concluded that professional money managers as a group do not do as well as the S&P 500. The article catered to the old, shopworn theory that throwing a dart at the *Wall Street Journal* yields better results than selective buying. The weakness of the article was that it combined all the money managers from mom-and-pop home operations having fewer than 20 clients with multibillion-dollar pension funds. There was no allowance for the expertise and experience of the managers or the risk and objectives of the managed funds. Individually managed funds were combined with pension funds and mutual funds.

Private pension funds and individually managed funds are under no obligation to make their results public. For this reason, I know of no valid data available to compare them. Since mutual funds must report publicly in a standard, regulated manner, meaningful comparisons are made. The *Mutual Fund Fact Book*, a publication of the Investment Company Institute, points out, using both five- and ten-year periods, that mutual funds have exceeded the rate of inflation and the overall market return as measured by the S&P 500.

The S&P 500 is a valid yardstick to measure management results. When selecting professional money management, demand a historical performance consistently superior to the S&P 500 Stock Index. Approach the process with the same dedication as selecting a physician, attorney, or any other professional. The record shows there are money managers who have demonstrated the ability to outperform the market.

All funds furnish literature that accurately discloses their individual performance. The key, however, is to relate that performance to some reliable index or indexes that show how well your investment has performed relative to similar investments.

For example, *Forbes* cites the 1985 total return of a large growth fund as 22 percent. This could be an impressive number. But as *Forbes* explains, this was "not nearly as good as the 28 percent gain of the average growth fund according to Lipper Analytical Services." In a further comparison with Johnson's Charts "Performance Report" (period ending December 31, 1985), the Dow Jones Industrial Average gained 32.8 percent, and Standard & Poor's 500 Composite Stock Index, 31.1 percent. Here again, both of these indexes outperformed the otherwise impressive 22 percent gain. Even though isolated results may be completely accurate, they bear little significance unless they are superior to other accepted indexes. More importantly, they must be consistently superior.

Since mutual funds are long-term investments, the isolated performance of several months or even a year in a good economic environment should not be the sole basis of investing. In order to intelligently appraise the risk and consistent performance of management, it's necessary to evaluate several years of operating results. Again, I suggest a minimum of at least five years.

Where Do I Get Information on Mutual Funds?

Most professional groups have an independent organiza-tion that represents the profession, gathers and records common data, and acts as its spokesperson. For the mu-tual fund industry, this organization is the Investment Company Institute. When you read about mutual funds in major newspapers and financial publications, the sta-tistical data often comes from the ICI.

The institute was founded in 1941 as the National Association of Investment Companies but later changed its name to the Investment Company Institute. Its objec-tive is to represent member mutual funds, shareholders, investment advisers, and underwriters. This covers a wide range of financial matters, from legislation, regulation, and taxation to statistics, economic information, and market research. The institute also functions as the clear-inghouse to which the public and the media may turn for information and advertising.

As part of its information service, each year the institute publishes The *Mutual Fund Fact Book*. This is an impartial, informative chronicle of data for both profes-sional and private investors. It begins with a review of previous years' economic growth or decline. Easy-to-read charts compare month-to-month changes in interest rates, inflation, and stock prices. And for the novice investor, there's a simple explanation of mutual funds.

Statistical data, accompanied by charts, show a breakdown of funds by numbers and investment objec-tives. Further into the book is a complete review of where mutual fund assets are invested, with the recent and historical trends in each category.

Of particular interest is the section dealing with the purchase of mutual funds. Here readers are introduced to the relationship between the dealer and the investor, and the fund and the investor. The Fact Book dispels the myth that mutual funds are only for individual investors when it shows the growth in mutual fund holdings among banks, corporations, fiduciaries, employee pension and profit-sharing plans, insurance companies, foundations, and other institutions. The retirement market is also analyzed, focusing on the various types of retirement plans that can be easily and conveniently funded with mutual fund shares. Federal regulations and current taxation on mutual fund shares are explained too. Finally, the Fact Book offers a complete glossary of mutual fund terms.

For anyone wanting complete and accurate information on mutual funds, the mutual fund industry, or both, the Investment Company Institute is an excellent source. Much of the statistical data in this book is used with permission of the ICI. It was selected because it is current, accurate, and unbiased toward any mutual fund or fund group. Information may be received by writing directly to Investment Company Institute, 1600 M Street, NW, Washington, DC 20036, or calling (202) 293-7700.

Endnote

[1] Income-oriented funds invest for income over growth. These funds may invest in bonds, preferred stocks, or high-dividend stocks.

CHAPTER 3

SELECTING THE RIGHT MUTUAL FUND: OR, HOW DO I FIND A SHOE THAT FITS?

> Make three correct guesses consecutively
> and you will establish a reputation as an expert.
> —*Lawrence Peter*

A few years ago I was into jogging. I can't understand why, since I'm not into masochism. But like all experiences, jogging taught me several valuable lessons. I remember two. Get shoes that fit *and* are designed for jogging.

I started with an excellent pair of tennis shoes that had chased balls with me for years. My first hint of incompatibility was a sore knee. The mutiny advanced to my lower back. One day at lunch, I was bemoaning the curse of old age with a fellow jogging addict.

"Are the knees the first to go?" I asked.

"They shouldn't be. What kind of shoes do you wear?"

"Good tennis shoes," I answered.

"Good" didn't impress him, but the tennis shoe confession grabbed his attention.

"You might as well be running in wing tip shoes!"

I didn't tell him I knew a broker who might also suggest that.

"You gotta get the right shoe—carefully designed especially for your purpose."

My friend went on to explain the importance of special purpose equipment, proper fit, and, most importantly, putting it all together. It all sounded so confusing I took up swimming. Now all I need is water. That always fits.

Looking back I see that the suggestion to match the proper equipment with the proper sport is good advice for any purpose. As a matter of fact, proper match is vital when selecting a mutual fund.

Once you identify your goal, the next step is to find several funds with investment objectives and risk latitude matching your own. From these funds begin your study for a final selection. But before the answers, the questions...

Be Concerned with Investment Goals

At one time selecting a mutual fund was a relatively simple matter. Today, however, there are a multitude of different mutual funds competing for your investment dollars. In fact, mutual funds alone outnumber all of the securities listed on the New York Stock Exchange.

While mutual funds are very popular now, most of their growth has taken place within the last decade. According to the Investment Company Institute, the number of funds has increased roughly fivefold in the past 10 years from 564 in 1980 to approximately 3,000 in 1989 (Appendix 1). The number is still growing.

Mutual funds were originally designed to help small investors. By pooling their money to create large institutional-type accounts, they could benefit from public professional management. These aren't get-rich-quick schemes but long-range investment plans. You pay an admission fee and a small percentage of the assets each year to the professionals who manage the fund, then you sit back and participate in the economy.[1]

Those who have patience with well-selected mutual funds have seen their assets grow through the years. It's not uncommon to see conservative mutual funds compound at an average of 12 to 13 percent a year over a period of 20, 30, or 50 or more years.

Unlike those who invested in mutual funds in the past, investors are now forcing a new challenge on the mutual fund industry—one the industry may have brought on itself. The cry is for short-term performance. Some funds have successfully answered it to this point. But keep in mind that trees don't grow to the sky.

Forbes recently pointed out that the average age of portfolio managers of one giant mutual fund group is 36. Several of their *sector funds*, those investing only in a specified industry, are managed by recent master's degree graduates as young as 26.

I don't wish to suggest one must be older to wisely pick stocks. An important part of managing money, however, is not only picking stocks and making profits in a good market but also protecting both assets and profits in a bad market. Some of today's mutual fund managers have never seen a bad market.

To some this argument may appear overconservative. If these are your feelings and you're comfortable in the fast lane with a new generation of money managers, you've a lot of company and a lot of funds from which to choose.

The *1987 Mutual Fund Fact Book* reported that "in 1975 mutual funds fit neatly into seven major categories." Ten years later those seven had grown to fifteen, with many funds further defining their investment objectives according to industry sectors, geographic limitations, or business philosophies. Today there are at least 22 or more different categories of mutual funds.

Mutual funds have seen tremendous changes. The important point is they are still basically long-term investments. Investors who buy mutual funds with long-term goals generally reach these goals with a minimum of surprises. Quick and unreasonable gains in mutual funds can happen, but they generally aren't consistent, and they don't last forever.

Of the hundreds of mutual funds offered to the public, how do you select the right one? Go back to your investment goals. What do you want? Where are you comfortable? What risks, if any, do you want to take? There are important questions to answer before selecting a mutual fund. Once you answer them, all that remains is to find the fund that fits.

The answer to that is in the prospectus. It's seldom on the best-seller list, so...

Why Do I Have to Spend All That Time Reading a Prospectus?

Before investing in any mutual fund, read the prospectus. It's required that you get one, so if it's not offered, ask!

Open it. It's not complicated. It's your protection contract. It tells about the fund. If you plan to own the fund, you'll want to know how your money will be treated.

Over the years I've developed a bad habit of buying unassembled merchandise: grills, swing sets, and so on. You name it, I've bought it.

What's worse, I try to assemble these things without first reading the instructions. Skinned knuckles and a bruised ego send me back to the instruction book, where I should have started. The bright side is that usually no real harm is done. The thing eventually comes together.

A similar story developed one day in October of 1987. A lot of investors had put together a financial plan using mutual funds. The stock market had enjoyed almost five years of uninterrupted euphoria, moving up with few corrections.

Most mutual funds had shared this prosperity. Their numbers were astounding. Johnson's Charts, an independent quarterly report on mutual fund performance, showed the average aggressive growth fund up more than 180 percent in less than six years.

Of course, anyone would choose that over the stodgy old income fund that was up only 138 percent. Well, maybe not, if the investor had first taken the time to read the instructions—that is, the prospectus.

The prospectus is a blueprint of the fund. It tells what the fund managers can and cannot do with your money. It describes risk and limits how much risk the fund is allowed to take. It tells you whether the purpose of the fund is to make profits as quickly as possible or to make only reasonable gains while first bringing in income and protecting your principal.

All these things you learn from the prospectus. However, in a hurry to reach a goal, sometimes anxious investors take the shortcut of not reading the instructions. With investing this can hurt. For example, let's look at several funds managed by one of the oldest and largest mutual fund management groups.

For more than 50 years they have managed funds, from the most conservative to the very aggressive. The investment objective of each is fully disclosed in that particular fund's prospectus. The numbers in the examples are important only because they show the relation between risk and reward. If the fund's prospectus says they are investing primarily for capital gains, then it is reasonable to expect more-than-average risk in an unfriendly stock market. On the other hand, funds that invest for income generally do not lose that income even though their stocks may suffer temporary market loss.

Beginning at the time the stock market reached its high on August 25, 1987, through October, 1987 the month it took its greatest fall, their fund that suffered the greatest loss was off 24.5 percent (the Dow was down 26.3 percent, and Standard & Poor's 500 lost 24.7 percent). However, this same fund was one of their top performers for the period of January 1982 through September 1987 and showed a gain of more than 260 percent.

That's the objective of the fund. They proclaim this in the prospectus: "Investment objective is to increase its shareholders' capital and income return over the years." Being directed to growth, it is reasonable that the fund is also exposed to greater risk when the market eventually corrects.

This firm's fund experienced the smallest loss, 11.1 percent, during the unprecedented market drop. This was less than half the loss of the overall market. Again, the shareholders should not be surprised, because the prospectus clearly states, "Investment objective is to emphasize current income while secondarily striving to attain capital growth." Investing for growth comes only after their primary income objective is reached.

Yet with all these warnings in the prospectus, many investors are amazed if their funds lose value. In most cases these investors do not take the time to read the fund's prospectus. They buy, or are sold, performance.

Performance is an easy trap in a bull market. After all, things are going up. Why worry about protection on the way down? The fact is, there has always been and will always be market corrections. The prudent investor protects against these down markets.

Read the prospectus before investing. Clearly see the fund's objective. Armed with this information, you can evaluate risk.

Like the assembly instructions with your outdoor grill, the prospectus is not designed to be entertaining. But just like those instructions, the prospectus carefully prepares you for what lies ahead. Ignore either, and you often wind up with a basket full of surprises.

How Great a Return Can I Expect?

A client recently remarked to me how he wished his father had had the foresight to invest $1,000 for him in his favorite stock 50 years ago. "I bet I'd be rich today," he figured.

I wondered how rich he would be. With a little research we were both surprised. One thousand dollars invested in his pet stock would be worth about $3,300 today. That's an increase of about 230 percent. On a compounded annual rate of return, however, the return is less than 2.5 percent a year. My friend wouldn't be quite as rich as he thought.

While addressing a group of investment brokers, Ted Jones, the senior partner of Jones Financial Companies, pointed out the unreasonable expectations investors sometimes dream of. "Often an investor expects money to grow and compound every year at a rate of 25, 30, and even 50 percent—and do it consistently." To illustrate the folly of such wishful thinking, Mr. Jones put a simple pocket calculator to some performance figures on the 30 stocks which make up the Dow Jones Industrial Average. He hypothetically invested $1,000 on December 31, 1933, in each of the Dow 30 stocks and checked their value 50 years later. A $1,000 investment in the top-performing stock grew to $990,000. That's a gain of 98,900 percent. The same investment in the poorest performer was worth only $1,725 at the end of the period. That's a gain of only 73 percent. The interesting point was that the compounded annual rate of return for the top stock was 14.8 percent a year; for the bottom stock, 1.1 percent. Yet these companies represented in the Dow are some of the largest, best-managed, and most-widely owned corporations in the world. The lesson is that it is unrealistic to expect grossly superior investment results.

Comparing this to one mutual fund management group over the same 50-year period, a hypothetical $1,000 investment in their fund would have grown into a portfolio worth $374,730. That's a compounding rate of 12.6 percent a year. Only three stocks on the Dow did better. Twenty-seven didn't do as well. Those are good numbers to support professional management through mutual funds.

If you select your own stocks or let a mutual fund do it for you, look for reasonable results.

What About Magazine Ratings of Mutual Funds?

Each year financial magazines compare mutual funds by past performances. The ranking can be a beneficial guide to the informed or a confusing recommendation to the uninformed.

Each editor uses his own guidelines to rate mutual funds. The result is that as you page through the various financial magazines in search of the "word," you discover there is none. Each magazine compiles a wealth of statistics to document its conclusions. But what do they say? A growth fund is superior to an income fund? That's like saying an apple is tastier than an orange. Every investment should stand on its own merit and not be arbitrarily grouped without concern for its underlying purpose or investment objective.

In the prospectus each mutual fund states its investment objectives and risk. For example, if a fund's objective is to provide regular income to investors, there is little chance, or reason, for it to be a top performer. In this case performance is inconsistent with the risk and purpose that the fund's shareholders choose to take.

When comparing funds many magazines consider the total return (the price gain plus reinvested dividends and capital gain distributions of the fund) but ignore the purpose of the fund. Since the price gain represents the rise in market value not yet taken from the fund's shares, this gain can disappear in an unfriendly market. All magazines should recognize this vulnerability to market conditions when analyzing mutual fund long-term stability. More are beginning to do this.

There are two fundamental tests in selecting a fund. One is the *consistency* of results. The other is the *continuity* of the people managing the fund. Simply put, the same managers must be consistent in making you money. If you do not know the managers and their long-term record, you could be in big trouble with last year's hot pick.

To appreciate the absolute necessity of management stability, look at the lessons of the late 1960s. With the Dow advancing almost unbroken from a low of 561 in June 1962 to a closing high of 969 in December 1965, many investors and some money managers began to believe trees grew to the sky. During that period of generally rising stock prices, profits came easy. Some mutual fund managers built reputations as "Golden Boys of Wall Street." But in late 1968 and early 1969, when the market began its dramatic correction to the 600 level on the Dow, some Golden Boys began to tarnish.

Each year readers anxiously wait to see whether their favorite mutual fund made the winner's circle. But although polls and ratings may be a way to increase magazine sales, readers can be misled if they take them too seriously.

The 1989 *Forbes* Annual Fund Ratings, for example, were particularly disturbing, because the magazine disqualified an entire mutual fund management group to introduce a new rating system that included only single-manager funds. That means that regardless of how outstanding or consistent the performance of any fund, if the spotlight was shared by more than one manager, that fund could not earn a trophy.

The editors admitted in explaining their system that they had snubbed an entire group of "excellent funds" (which they named) simply because these funds were not managed by a single star. Then they admitted that their top pick probably would lose its luster if the manager pursued other career opportunities. Oddly enough, several months after the annual rating was released, the manager resigned. What were they rating, a mutual fund or an individual?

One of the management groups excluded from the honor roll in favor of the best one-person-acts has been on the honor roll every year since its inception. In fact, the group would have had more entries on the honor roll in 1989 than any other fund group.

Funds managed by this group met or exceeded this magazine's two most important criteria for evaluating mutual fund performance: efficiency and total return. Over meaningful periods of time—10 years or more— every single one of the common-stock funds managed by this organization outperformed the U.S. market as a whole. That's consistency you can take to the bank. But none of these funds are managed by a single person. Portions of each fund's assets are assigned to different individuals, who manage those assets as if they were an entire fund. This would appear to provide added protection should one of the individuals have an off year or resign.

There have been numerous articles written on the hazards of a single superstar money manager. History tells it best. Mutual fund ratings can be fun to read, but there could be danger in taking them too seriously.

The letters to *Forbes* (including one from this reporter) pointed out the fallacy of such arbitrary exclusion of any mutual fund or fund group. Obviously the number of protests prompted Forbes (much to their credit) to reconsider. In their September 1990 Fund Ratings, they gave prominent space to partially retracting their previous "portfolio designed by a committee" bias. "The rule that committees make poor fund managers has a dramatic exception," *Forbes* admits. "Here's a camel that runs like a horse."

This example is provided neither to whet your appetite for a particular fund nor to disparage a highly respected financial publication like *Forbes*. My purpose is that you should know what you expect of your mutual fund and be knowledgeable enough to see whether you are getting it. Don't be led blindly by any magazine to decide what is best for you...even if they are highly respected.

Should I Choose More Than One Fund?

Two reasons to choose mutual funds are diversification and diversification.

You're not seeing double. It simply means that spreading risk is often the most important factor in an investment program.

For this reason, many investors choose mutual funds that offer a diversified portfolio of 100 or more individual securities. This often satisfies the diversification requirement.

But is it still possible to lose principal even when spreading risk? Unfortunately, yes. While many mutual funds offer a meaningful history of consistently positive results, none guarantee future performance. But diversification among mutual funds can increase the safety factor.

To illustrate, all you need is a current Standard & Poor's *Stock Guide*, available at most New York Stock Exchange member firms. In the back is a mutual fund summary with a wealth of statistical information. One fund column shows what $10,000 invested as of a particular date (usually five or more years) is worth today. That's all that's needed for the diversification game.

Before beginning any multi-fund diversification program, however, understand two points. First, plan on leaving your money invested for at least five years. Second, diversify into at least five different mutual funds.

Using these guidelines, we hypothetically placed $10,000 in each of our five favorite mutual funds. All are managed by the same family of funds. Although this is not necessary, it does offer the benefit of discounted charges and swapping privileges. It also prevented us from using 20/20 hindsight and selecting only the best-performing funds. For simplification we chose only middle-of-the-road growth and income funds.

Table 3-1	
Selected Funds	
Fund # 1	$ 25,359
Fund # 2	24,479
Fund # 3	23,271
Fund # 4	21,442
Fund # 5	23,029
	$117,580

Table 3-2	
Worst Performers	
Fund # 1	$13,449
Fund # 2	12,042
Fund # 3	16,171
Fund # 4	9,353
Fund # 5	10,019
	$61,034

Table 3-1 shows that a $10,000 investment made in each of five selected mutual funds on December 31, 1982, grew to $117,580.

Table 3-2 shows the value of the same $50,000 divided equally into the first five *worst* performing funds shown in the Stock Guide. That diversified investment grew to $61,034.

Although it offers no guarantee of future results, this little game does make a strong case for diversification.

Even if you had selected the five worst performing funds, your investment would have gained $11,034. Individually, one fund lost slightly and one was unchanged. But collectively they managed to produce a modest overall profit. That's the bad news.

The good news is that by doing your homework, a careful selection of diversified funds dedicated to your goals and risk tolerance can not only increase your safety factor but also offers the opportunity of reasonable financial rewards.

What Is Total Return?

Total return is a meaningful way to evaluate the progress of your investments and compare those results with the return on other investments with the same objective.

Total return is a percentage figure that shows changes in the value of your investments when reinvesting both income and capital results. Say you own a $50,000 managed portfolio of securities. During the year

$50,000		Beginning value
2,000	(4%)	Income (reinvested)
4,000	(8%)	Capital gain (reinvested)_
1,500	(3%)	Capital gain (unrealized)
$57,500		Year-end value
$ 7,500	(15%)	Annual total return

these securities produced dividend income of $2,000, which was then reinvested into the portfolio. More securities were sold, adding another $4,000 in capital gains, which was also reinvested. Finally, the value of securities in the portfolio increased by $1,500. At the end of the year, the portfolio is worth $57,500, up $7,500: that's 15 percent total return.

Remember, to be a true indication of performance, make sure your total return is over a meaningful period. Again, I suggest a minimum of five years. The key is consistency. Big gains followed by big losses are not a blueprint for success.

For example, look at the hypothetical five-year progress of an invested dollar. The first year it gains 20 percent; the next year it loses 50 percent. Years three and

Year	Erratic Compounding	Steady Compounding
1	$1.00	$1.00
	.20 + 20%	.12 +12%
	1.20	1.12
2	.60 –50%	.13 +12%
	/60	1.25
3	.30 +50%	.15 +12%
	.90	1.40
4	.45 +50%	.17 +12%
	1.35	1.57
5	.14 +10%	.19 +12%
	$1.49	$1.76

four produce 50 percent gains back-to-back, and the fifth year posts a respectable 10 percent gain. Not bad, you say. But believe it or not, with these erratic fluctuations, the original dollar was worth only $1.49 five years later. Compare this with the dull, steady compounding of 12 percent each year. Five years later, that dollar was worth $1.76.

Investment figures can be revealing, but they become even more meaningful when compared to other similar investments. In our example an erratic investment gained 49 percent in five years, whereas a steady investment showed a 76 percent gain. The immediate conclusion might be to always select the slow, steady route. But how did other investments perform during this same period? By prudently selecting investments with some growth potential, could you have done better? A visit to your library or brokerage office will get this information. You can find performance records that compare the Dow Jones Industrial Average, the S&P 500, the cost of living, money market instruments, hundreds of mutual funds, and more.

No matter what yardstick you choose to run against, if you find your total return coming up short, it is time to rethink your investment strategy.

What Is the Difference between Investment and Speculation?

The other day I came across a definition of investment opportunity as the point at which a fool and his money are parted. I assume it was intended to be funny. It wasn't.

Many would-be investors don't know the difference between investment opportunity and blind speculation. Such people, when parted from their money, are loudest to complain of investment risk. Unknowingly, perhaps, they aren't investing. They're speculating.

Most investments require some risk. It need not be speculative risk. For example, if you begin a small business venture of selling greeting cards in the home, you need some money to buy cards. If the worst happened— no sales—your only loss would be the money you invested to buy the cards. You know the risk and can reasonably predict your reward. This is investment. On the other hand, if you decided to take that same money and place a bet on a favorite pony, this is speculation. It's still speculation if you forget the horses and put the money on a fly-by-night stock.

Once you accept the difference between speculation and investing, it becomes clear that investing dollars in carefully selected mutual funds is a reasonable way to participate in the growth of the economy. That's why more individual investors are looking to mutual funds as an alternative to savings accounts or certificates of deposit.

According to the *Mutual Fund Fact Book*, there are approximately 25,000 securities issues traded on the organized exchanges and the over-the-counter markets. Together they have an estimated value of more than $2 trillion. Of these, mutual funds have investments in at least 10,000 equity securities (common and preferred stocks) totaling more than $74 billion. They own bonds of over 3,000 corporations, accounting for an additional $26.5 billion. This gives some indication of the tremendous investment made in the future growth of this country.

Bernard Baruch, the renowned financier, best cautioned against speculation in his autobiography, *Baruch: My Own Story*. "Don't speculate unless you can make it a full-time job. Beware of barbers, beauticians, waiters—or anyone—bringing gifts of 'inside' information."

Investment versus speculation. It's a difference that could decide your financial success.

Endnote

[1] Chapter 7, "Mutual Fund Costs," discusses load funds, no-load funds, and various costs.

Chapter 4

INVEST WITH A PLAN: OR, WHERE DID MY MONEY GO?

> It takes 80 years to make an
> overnight success.
> —*Eddie Cantor*

Should My Investment Plans Change with My Life Circumstances?

I had the opportunity to visit with Jack Phelan, a general partner of Edward D. Jones & Company. Unlike many of his Wall Street peers, Mr. Phelan didn't learn investing from a paneled office high above the city. He met investors on the farms and rural communities around St. Louis. He knows where conservative, hardworking folks want to put their money. They told him over coffee at the kitchen table.

He told me about a long-time friend who recently sold his business and retired. The business was very successful, so even after taxes this 66-year-old gentleman had a generous sum of money to invest. "I was somewhat surprised, but genuinely delighted, when he told me how he had chosen to invest for his retirement," Mr. Phelan said. During his working years his friend had generally limited his investments to mutual funds investing for long-term growth with current income secondary. "The funds performed well and accomplished what they were bought for. So, when he told me he had divided the proceeds from the sale of his business between insured tax-free bonds and U.S. government securities, I was surprised...and delighted." Mr. Phelan explained, "Often folks who have been exposed to the risk of business all their life will continue this philosophy into retirement."

The story of how this businessman shifted from the working/building years to the retirement/enjoyment years is a lesson from which we should all benefit. Each stage of life offers a different challenge to investment planning. During the working years, our friend was concerned with building capital. He invested in his business, and his surplus dollars went into other growth businesses through investment in common stocks through a fully managed mutual fund. Once he reached retirement age, his goals changed. What he wanted now was safe, reliable income to help him enjoy what he had earned. The time for taking risks had passed.

"He selected long-term government securities because these offered the greatest safety with a generous income for many years to come," Mr. Phelan said. "Since he is still in a very high tax bracket, tax-exempt bonds make a lot of sense. He further satisfied his safety needs by investing only in insured bonds. In this case he chose an insured tax-free trust as the vehicle."

How did he now view the mutual funds that he owned? Mr. Phelan explained that his friend still liked the idea of some growth to combat inflation. Since the fund had a long record of increasing dividends, he requested that all dividends now be paid to him, rather than reinvested as had been done during the growth years. He is convinced that these dividends will continue to grow, providing him with a rising income to meet the rising cost of living.

His investment portfolio is almost equally divided—about a third each in an insured tax-free trust, U.S. government-guaranteed securities, and an old-friend mutual fund that has served him well. He did set aside about 5 percent of these assets into a money market fund that credits daily current interest. Additionally, it offers instant liquidity of check writing without penalty. Although all his investments could be sold on any business day, he does not intend to disturb those. He feels comfortable having ready cash available for an emergency.

"It's a super story of what planned, long-term, conservative investing can do," Mr. Phelan concluded. As I looked at this conservative midwesterner who helped mold the philosophy of his investment firm, I couldn't help but think, He knows of what he speaks.

Mr. Phelan told a story of a plan. His friend's goals may be different from yours, and his investments may not suit your needs, but the moral of the story is planning—how as life changes, needs change; and a well-designed plan is flexible enough to meet those changing needs.

So, there is an answer to our concern...

How Can I Change My Investments as My Needs Change?

Mutual funds are many things to many people. They tell you about it in the investment objectives of the prospectus (Chapter 3).

If you select a family of funds—one group which manages several mutual funds with different objectives—a transfer within the group is simple and accomplished at little or no cost.

For example, some retired people who enjoyed a fund's benefit of growth and income during their working years may now find a 5 percent or 6 percent dividend little better than the income from their savings account.

Their present need is more income, more safety of principal, and less growth.

An income or bond fund could offer a reasonable alternative. By investing in a bond fund, they might increase their income to 10 percent or more. On a $100,000 investment this could mean enjoying a monthly check of as much as $800, compared with $500 or less at the lower rate. In addition, the couple is still comfortable with the knowledge that their investment continues to be professionally managed by the same managers they have grown to trust over the years. Many folks select income-oriented mutual funds when they have a need for more spendable dollars.

Here again, a word of caution is in order. A mutual fund that deals in senior securities (bonds) and pays a high current income is not a guarantee of safety and security. The key, as with all mutual funds, is management integrity and consistency.

The integrity and consistency of a fund's manager can be determined only through research. Look at the fund record. There are several independent companies that specialize in researching mutual funds. Compare the fund's results with those of other mutual funds with the same investment objective. See how the fund's managers have done in the past year, five years, and longer. The information is available, but you have to make the effort to find it and study it. Your public library can usually assist you in getting the information. If it is not available, try contacting one of these professional services for subscription information.

1. Weisenberger Investment Company
   Division of Warren, Gorham & Lamont
   1633 Broadway
   New York, New York 10019

2. Lipper Analytical Securities Corporation
   74 Trinity Place
   New York, New York 10006
3. Johnson's Charts
   69 Delaware
   Suite 604
   Buffalo, New York 14202
4. CDA Investment Technologies
   11501 Georgia Avenue
   Silver Springs, Maryland 20902

All investments have some risk. The more risk, the more the borrower must pay the investor to take that risk. Some funds pay very high income by investing in securities of questionable quality. And even though the fund is restricted to investments in senior securities, there could be considerable risk attached, which explains the higher income. In these cases the managers have chosen to sacrifice some safety for more income.

If your investment is for income to meet daily living expenses, it is essential that that income be dependable. Regardless of the income promised today, it is of little value if reduced or stopped tomorrow. When investing for income, also satisfy the need for safety. Ask about risk, and make sure you get answers.

When economic times are good and the stock market is going up, you may decide to "gamble a little" and set aside a good financial plan for a "piece of the action." When the dust settles, a "piece of the action" often translates into "I want to win."

Back in 1982, when the stock market began to recover from a 17-year seesaw ride between 500 and 1,000 on the Dow, I had a client with family money invested for safety and income. The total return on the investment averaged more than 11 percent. But that year some mutual funds advanced as much as 50 percent. Of course, they were growth funds that paid little or no dependable income. They were unsuitable for any investor who needed safety and regular income. In spite of this, the client wanted to know...

Why Not Just Bet on the Fund with the Highest Rate of Return?

For more than 19 years, the New Orleans Saints lost football games. They were the only team in the NFL without a winning season. I've seen the Saints build an impressive lead, and give it away. Almost certain winning situations were sacrificed for the sparkle of the big play that didn't come. That's consistency! But demonstrate that kind of consistency with your investments, and they probably won't last 19 years.

The Capital Guardian Group, internationally recognized for professional money management, manages assets of approximately $9 billion, representing the holdings of more than 650,000 shareholders. They recently published some eye-opening comparisons on the necessity of protecting your investments during difficult times.

Although it's important to make profits in good times, it's equally important to protect capital in bad times. For example, assume an investment gains 15 percent for three years in a row. That's an average annual compound return of 15 percent. In the fourth year, a market reversal drives the investment to a 15 percent loss. Now the average rate of return for the four-year period has dropped to 6.6 percent. To get back to the 15 percent average annual rate of return enjoyed before the setback, this investment must gain a whopping 56 percent in the fifth year.

According to a study made by the Capital Guardian Group, "It isn't unusual for a fund to drop 15 percent or more in a single year. In fact, it's happened 698 times over the past 15 years. But, gaining at least 56 percent in any one year is much harder. That's happened only 60 times during the same period."

Further, the study points out that with more aggressive investments that show as much as a 25 percent average annual compound rate of return for a consecutive three-year period, a fourth-year 25 percent setback would require the fifth year to produce a 108 percent gain in order to recover the 25 percent average! The study found annual drops of 25 percent or more occurring 347 times in 15 years. But in this same period, only three times, "all in 1979, and all highly volatile gold funds," did funds go up at least 108 percent.

The message is clear. With any investment that has benefits from capital gains, it's important to protect those gains during the period of correction that's almost certain to come. If the drop is severe, as it often is in cases where the gain has been unusually rapid, the time of recovery to your average annual rate of return can be long.

The December 31, 1974, edition of *Wiesenberger's Mutual Fund Management Results* provides a prime example. Wiesenberger is a nationally recognized research company that specializes in statistical data on mutual funds—no sales pitch and no gloss, just numbers.

The year 1974 brought back the results of risk in the stock market for both high-rolling and conservative money managers. It proved once again the importance of looking for reasonable investment results in good times and downside protection in bad times. This may sound simple, but it's easy to get carried away in the euphoria of a bull market. Greed, the mistaken illusion that trees can grow to the sky, often impairs better judgment.

Let's take a look at 1974 and play "what-if." What if you had invested in a "maximum capital gain" mutual fund at the beginning of 1974? Maximum capital gain funds usually look for stocks to give fast profits. Dividend income is considered incidental. This offers risk. Of the 98 such funds Wiesenberger Services reported in 1974, only one showed a gain. The average fund lost 27.7 percent.

What if you had invested in high-flying performance during these years? If you were in the fast lane and willing to take a loss, you probably did. If you invested in one of these mutual funds looking to get rich quick with little or no risk, you faced an unwelcome surprise and a quick depletion of your investment dollars.

Looking at the five-year period of 1970 through 1974, the average loss was 36.9 percent. There's no doubt these were difficult years in the stock market. In 1970 the Dow Jones Industrial Average hovered around 600. In 1972 it briefly broke the then-magic 1,000 mark, only to begin a steady downturn about the time of our first energy crisis. By the end of 1974 it was back where it started.

In contrast to the fast-moving performance funds, the more conservative growth and income funds continued to pay their shareholders dividends during these difficult times. In many cases those dividends even increased. Of course these funds lost share value, but the investors who reinvested their dividends benefited by purchasing depressed shares at bargain prices. When the market eventually turned around, all shares, including the bargain buys, increased in value.

Those investors who bought mutual funds with reasonable expectations and had patience were able not only to survive those difficult times but also to prosper in good times.

While it may be tempting to buy a risky mutual fund to get rich quick, don't be shortsighted. The lessons of investing can well be compared to the age-old story of the tortoise and the hare. The consistent, patient advance of the tortoise in the end beat the spasmodic, irregular performance of the hare.

Of course, I realize that not everyone is interested in safety and income. Some are willing to take that extra chance with the hope of bigger rewards. For those who understand investment risk and are willing to accept it, a logical question is...

Can I Have Results Now?

Since mutual funds are designed as long-term (more than five years) investments, you should not be concerned with daily activity. Focus on long-term performance. A mutual fund is bought to build financial assets for future goals like education, retirement, or even a cabin on the lake. It's not intended to provide quick, overnight profits.

Mutual fund managers know, however, that many investors still want some money working aggressively. Sure, they realize there's more risk this way, but they also know with risk comes the possibility of reward. For these folks, there are mutual funds whose objective is maximum capital gain.

The managers of aggressive funds are more interested in companies on the threshold of growth than established companies paying generous dividends. They look for promising companies that, in the judgment of the fund's managers, will survive and grow into industry leaders. Since such companies generally have a limited history of performance, the risk of owning them is greater than the risk of investing in companies with proven results. On the other hand, prudent selection could bring excellent rewards by recognizing early investment potential. Most of our largest corporations started small.

The important thing about seeking maximum capital gains is that you realize growth is usually the only reward. Growth-oriented companies dedicate the bulk of their earnings to expansion. In most cases they borrow, sometimes at high interest rates, to finance research and development, growth and expansion. The result is there is not a lot left for dividends. So during periods of declining stock prices, these companies often suffer a greater market loss. Because you receive no dividend to cushion against capital erosion in poor times, you should expect a much greater growth potential in good times.

I continually stress that mutual funds are long-term investments. The reason is that an aggressive, growth-oriented fund may produce outstanding results in good times, but it could be a financial debacle in a bad stock market. An impressive gain followed by a greater loss still puts you behind the starting point. In investing it's best not to play catch-up.

There are many aggressive mutual funds with good long-term results. Don't be deceived by short-term heroics.

Is There a Way to Protect Principal and Continue Growth?

Many investors dream of finding a way to protect their principal while still participating in the growth of their capital. In reality this isn't as difficult as it sounds. A little knowledge and reliance on the management of a reputable mutual fund could be the answer.

First, select a mutual fund family that has a conservative income fund and a growth fund. Next, make sure cross-investment of all income dividends is allowed.

The idea is to invest in the income fund and then reinvest all dividend payments in the growth fund. This way, your original principal remains in a fund with the objective of protecting your assets. The earnings, by being reinvested more aggressively, have the potential for faster growth. In addition, the dividends that are reinvested on a regular, systematic basis offer the advantage of dollar cost averaging.

I played the what-if game using a family of funds with more than 50 years of consistent results. For conservative income I selected a fund that the Mutual Fund Values rating service placed on its list of 5 percent least-risky equity funds. The fund has posted 15 consecutive years of positive results. Lipper Analytical Services shows the fund had, in the past 10 years, a total return of 332 percent. These numbers are not only impressive but also met my criterion for safety of principal.

For the growth fund, in which the dividends from my income fund would be invested, I selected one of this group's star performers, with a 10-year gain of 498 percent.

Someone who did this with $100,000 about 10 years ago would now have almost half a million dollars. Here's how it works.

By taking only the income from my conservative fund over the past 10 1/2 years, I periodically would have reinvested a total of $114,734 into my growth fund. That would have grown to $294,097. At the same time my principal in the conservative income fund would have grown to $204,289. The total value of the funds—$498,386.

The key, of course, is doing serious homework to select your income and your growth funds. Granted, I enjoyed the benefits of statistical hindsight, but this process of historical performance selection is the only valid way I know.

Obviously, no system can guarantee a profit. The past 10 years was a period of generally rising stock prices. No one can predict the results of future performance, but a careful study of a fund's management and its long-term performance under various economic conditions should give you a big advantage over the dart throwers.

Here's another way you might have your cake and eat it too. So far we've talked about investing lump sums of money into one or more mutual funds. If you happen to have the money and don't plan on needing it for immediate expenses, this makes a lot of sense. But for most of us large sums of investment dollars are few and far between. So what's the answer? Either invest when you do have surplus funds or budget regular investments as part of your financial plan. This is the "get-rich-slowly" theory.

Why Should I Invest a Few Bucks Each Month?

Everyone knows that a sure way to get rich is to buy when prices are low and sell when they are high. One lady was so convinced of this theory that when she brought in some stock to sell, she placed a limit order. She heard that a limit order placed a minimum price, or limit, on the amount she would accept for the stock.

"What limit would you like to put on your sale?" I asked.

"Oh," she replied, "sell it when it gets as high as it's going."

Of course, most of us realize it's impossible to know how high the price of a stock will rise or how low it can fall. So rather than buying common stocks or mutual fund shares on the basis of investment value, some become discouraged because they can't "beat the market." To those, take heart. There is a way to beat the market. It's called *dollar cost averaging*.

Like any winning formula, dollar cost averaging requires a little knowledge, a lot of discipline, and a regular amount of money available for investing. The amount of money is immaterial. Whether you select $100 or $1,000 a month to invest, the important thing is that the same amount is available each month. The basis of dollar cost averaging is that no mutual fund always goes up or down. Like the market, each fluctuates. By ignoring the fluctuations and keeping to the discipline of regular deposits, you eliminate the temptation of trying to pick the bottom or the top. Your only concern is regular investments at regular intervals. Since the market value of mutual fund shares fluctuates, your regular investment buys more shares when prices are low and fewer shares when prices are higher.

For example, using $100 a month, here is how dollar cost averaging works in all market conditions (Table 4-1).

In all three market conditions *your average cost per share* is $8.57, yet the *average market price per share* is

---

Table 4-1
Dollar Cost Averaging

In a Rising Market

Month	Deposit	Share Price	Shares Bought
June	$100	$ 5	20
July	100	10	10
August	100	20	5
Total	$300	—	35

Average Cost per Share $8.57 ($300 divided by 35 shares)

In a Falling Market

Month	Deposit	Share Price	Shares Bought
September	$100	$20	5
October	100	10	10
November	100	5	20
Total	$300	—	35

Average Cost per Share $8.57 ($300 divided by 35 shares)

In a Fluctuating Market

Month	Deposit	Share Price	Shares Bought
December	$100	$ 5	20
January	100	20	5
February	100	10	10
Total	$300	—	35

Average Cost per Share $8.57 ($300 divided by 35 shares)

$11.67 ($5 + $10 + $20, divided by 3 = $11.67). This is the little knowledge you need to begin dollar cost averaging. The important ingredient is discipline—regular deposits at regular intervals.

The carrot you are tempted to chase is the unattainable urge to buy low and sell high. The discipline of dollar cost averaging eliminates this myth and puts you on a solid foundation to beat the market.

There are variations to the dollar cost averaging plan. One effective way not only lets you benefit from systematic deposits on the way in but also protects you with systematic withdrawals on the way out. So...

How Can I Use Dollar Cost Averaging with a Lump Sum Investment?

The only certainty in the stock market is uncertainty. No one has yet been able to accurately predict market movement, direction, or timing and do it consistently.

The idea, of course, is to buy stock at bargain prices. Bargain buying is like buying your straw hat in winter. Not everyone will do this, so most are satisfied with reasonable prices.

One way to increase your chances of buying at a reasonable price is to use dollar cost averaging by investing in regular installments over the next year or two. Then, once you complete your planned investment, leave it where it is for at least five years before you begin withdrawals. By planning both payments and withdrawals over an extended period, you reduce your chances of major market surprises.

One mutual fund that aims for long-term growth and income illustrated this technique by using its investment experience over the past 38 years. You might ask your fund, or any fund you plan to buy, to do this for you using a simple computer illustration.

This mutual fund took $100,000 and invested it over an 18-month period beginning January 1973, the top of a bull market. Five years after beginning the first installment, the account had grown to more than $148,000.

At this point the shareholders began regular withdrawals of 8 percent. The first year withdrawals amounted to $11,877. The following year the principal had grown so that the same 8 percent withdrawal was $12,392. Last year the annual withdrawal was $29,310. By the end of 1987, 15 years after the program started, all withdrawals plus the remaining balance totaled more than $545,000, more than five times the amount invested.

The fund made calculations for each 15-year period since it began in 1950. Some results were better than others, but even in the worst case (1960—-1974), there was still $94,000 left after withdrawing $120,015.

The fund is quick to point out these are not guarantees. It does, however, make a strong case that a disciplined program of regular investments and withdrawals can provide the growing income most people will need in the future.

Dollar cost averaging is nothing new. The difference is that most dollar cost averaging is done with small, regular amounts over many years. Here, a lump sum is dedicated to investment over an extended time.

The dilemma is when to invest. For anyone afraid to jump into a volatile stock market with one lump sum, the advantages of spreading the investment over regular installments make sense. Once the decision is made, stick to your schedule. Otherwise you risk that impulse to outguess the market.

With installment investing you may not always buy your straw hat in winter, but you stand a good chance of getting a reasonable price. More importantly, your money probably will be there when you need it.

Next to the planned, regular investing approach of dollar cost averaging, the best estate-building tool you have is a silent worker called *compounding*.

What Happens If You Let Your Profits Ride?

Remember the magic of compounding, as presented in grade school? Remember how the teacher explained $10 in the bank earning 8 percent? At the end of a year it would grow to $10.80; so the next year that amount, earning the same 8 percent, would be worth $11.66; and on and on. The point was that you were earning interest on interest by letting it accumulate. It sounds simple now, but then it was a bear to understand.

The fact is, some investors today have forgotten the magic of compounding, even though it is still one of the most valuable tools in the accumulation of wealth. If you can manage to defer receiving income from investments and allow that income to accumulate and compound, your estate will benefit from that same magic of earning interest on interest.

Here's the power of compounding (Figure 4-1). Look at a $10,000 investment with no principal fluctuation. Reinvest the monthly income at the same 10 percent, and the original $10,000 nearly triples in 10 years— $27,070. The same $10,000 at simple interest (no interest earned on interest) grows to only $20,000 in the same 10 years. The power of compounding earns you another $7,000.

Stretch that to 20 years, and the numbers are more dramatic. By letting your monthly interest on $10,000 compound for 20 years, you earn a whopping $43,281 more than you would with simple interest. The point is that an investment from which all income is taken can earn only simple interest. In our example, if you withdraw the $1,000 annual interest, there remains only the original principal to earn interest. By leaving the interest to compound, you see the dramatic effect of wealth accumulation.

The second lesson illustrated (Figure 4-1) is the importance of selecting the highest available yield compatible with your safety requirements. As you see, $10,000 compounding monthly for 20 years at 12 percent ($108,926) more than doubles the value of the same investment compounding at 8 percent ($49,268).

The magic of compounding is always impressive, but you must be wondering...

Does It Make a Difference When I Begin?

One of the best friends any investor has is time. Time is more predictable than luck and easier to handle than success. Time works for you and charges nothing.

A simple time equation is worth considering. The more time you have, the less money you need to invest for the same goal. This is rather basic and generally gets little argument.

Putting numbers to this simple concept, however, can be alarming, particularly for those who let too much time pass them by.

Consider two individuals, both age 22. Investor A decides to begin a long-range investment program.

He selects a 10 percent fixed-income investment into which he deposits $2,000 a year. Eight years later, at age 30, he decides to stop his regular investments. He withdraws nothing and makes no further investments.

At age 65 he retires. By allowing time to work for him, his modest $16,000 investment, spaced over an eight-year period, has grown to $812,000.

Table 4-2 illustrates the growth of Investor A's account, with no investments after eight years.

Investor B, on the other hand, chooses not to begin his investment program until age 30, the same year Investor A stopped.

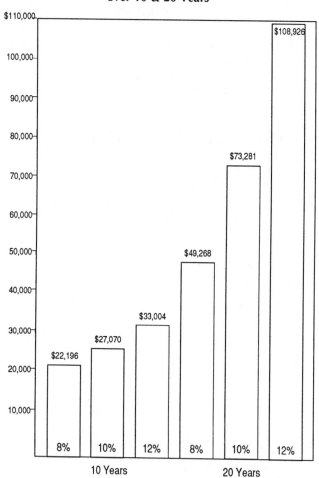

Figure 4-1
Compounding
Monthly Income Reinvested at 8%, 10% & 12%
over 10 & 20 Years

	Table 4-2	
	Investor A	
End of Year	Cumulative Annual Deposits	Total Value
1	$ 2,000	$ 2,208
8	16,000*	25,599
10	16,000	31,190
20	16,000	83,747
30	16,000	224,867
40	16,000	603,782
43	16,000	812,019

Investor A reached age 65 after beginning deposits 43 years ago.

* Stopped making deposits

For the next 35 years Investor B continues to deposit $2,000 a year into the same 10 percent fixed-income investment. At age 65 he retires. During those 35 years he invested $70,000, but his retirement account is worth only $653,000. That's $159,000 less than his counterpart.

Table 4-3 shows how a delay of only eight years requires more deposits and results in a much smaller reward.

Investor A invested only about 25 percent as much as Investor B, but when they both reached age 65, Investor A's investment was worth almost 25 percent more.

What's the difference? Time.

Investor A began an investment program early and let time take the modest annual deposits and begin the magic of compounding.

Investor B let time slip by for only eight years, but that short time delay was devastating in investment dollars needed and financial goals met.

Time can be your best friend or your worst enemy.

	Table 4-3	
	Investor B	
End of Year	**Cumulative Annual Deposits**	**Total Value**
1	$ 2,000	$ 2,208
8	20,000*	35,834
10	40,000	132,051
20	60,000	390,398
30	70,000	653,293

Investor B reached age 65 after beginning deposits 35 years ago.

When you're planning to invest, don't be a Scarlett O'Hara and "worry about it tomorrow."

When investing for long-term retirement or education, it's vital to prudently investigate the options. At one time there were limited investment choices for the individual. Today there are many investment products to answer your needs. Mutual funds are an ideal way to let dollar cost averaging, compounding, and time work for you.

Why Account for Inflation When Planning for Retirement?

A concern of most working people is whether they'll have enough money when they retire. The answer is more complex than it appears.

More than 900 retirees were surveyed by Maximilian E. Szinovacz, Ph.D., at Florida State University in 1984. His studies show that "a sizeable number of respondents not only failed to prepare for the income reduction retirement usually brings about, but did not even find out about their benefits."

So whether or not you'll have enough money when you retire depends on how you plan. It's just as important to plan for that money to last throughout retirement.

The time to answer these concerns is while there's still time to plan, not at retirement. Although the future offers no guarantees, some basic assumptions must be made in any financial plan. These assumptions use historical data for future planning. Any investment plan should be monitored regularly, and the progress evaluated. Make changes when necessary.

In his book *Financial Planning*, Loren Dunton, president of the National Center for Financial Education, devotes an entire chapter to retirement needs. Using age 65 for retirement and Social Security as the base, he estimates that "maintaining a standard of living after retirement not too much reduced from the best economic years" may be achieved at 50 to 60 percent of one's gross salary. A more realistic estimate is probably 70 to 75 percent. This is a figure most retirement planners suggest. Ideally retirement should mean more leisure time for travel and hobbies. Generally this cannot be done on half of one's working-years income. The objective, therefore, is to plan for spendable retirement income effectively equal to the working-years income. Additionally, more people are retiring, voluntarily or otherwise, before age 65. This reduces Social Security benefits and prolongs the time your retirement nest egg must continue to produce income.

Individuals have different needs, so use a retirement income that is comfortable for you. The consumer price index (CPI) since 1964 shows an average inflation rate of just over 6 percent. That's a reasonable figure to use in our projections.

Here are two simple illustrations. Table 4-4 shows how inflation at various rates erodes buying power over the years. For example, if you estimate your retirement expense today at $20,000 annually, using an inflation rate of 6 percent, in 10 years you'd need 1.79 times as

MUTUAL FUND MAGIC

Table 4-4
Inflation Effect on Buying Power

Years	4%	5%	6%	7%	8%	9%
5	1.22	1.28	1.34	1.40	1.47	1.54
10	1.48	1.63	1.79	1.97	2.16	2.37
20	2.19	2.65	3.87	3.87	4.66	5.60
30	3.24	4.32	7.61	7.61	10.06	13.27

Table 4-5
Monthly Investment Required
to Accumulate $1,000

Years	7%	8%	9%	10%	11%	12%
5	$13.97	$13.61	$13.26	$12.91	$12.58	$12.24
10	5.78	5.47	5.17	4.88	4.61	4.35
20	1.92	1.70	1.50	1.32	1.16	1.01
30	.89	.68	.55	.45	.36	.29

much, or about $35,800. Use your own figures, but Table 4-4 illustrates the need to plan inflation into your retirement.

Table 4-5 shows how much you must invest monthly at various rates of return to accumulate $1,000 over a given time. For example, for an investment compounding at 10 percent, about $4.88 per month will accumulate $1,000 in 10 years. If you want a retirement nest egg of $500,000, $2,440 each month is necessary to reach this goal in 10 years ($4.88 x 500 = $2,440). If retirement is 30 years away, about $225 each month ($.45 x 500 = $255) will meet your goal. Early planning can make your goal possible.

Once you reach retirement, these assets are used to produce the income necessary for a comfortable standard of living then and through future years.

The government frequently changes the rules of our retirement. Look at the major changes in IRAs and reductions of deductible contributions to pension plans and 401(k)s. Many people work with the fear that at or near retirement their employment could end. Forced early retirement has left many with disrupted plans because of reduced income. These concerns are sound reasons to consider what you can do to ensure a happy retirement when the time comes.

Even with all this planning, there's still an important question...

Can I Run Out of Money After Retirement?

As life expectancy increases, retirees become more concerned about outliving their money. How long will the money last?

If you know how much money you begin with, your annual withdrawal needs, and the total return on the balance, you can figure how long your nest egg will last. For example, referring to Table 4-6, you see that an investment from which you take 10 percent each year and that earns 9 percent on the balance lasts 26 years. If you live longer, you outlive your money.

If accumulating a larger retirement fund is not possible, you must either decrease your annual income or increase your return on investment. From a purely mathematical standpoint, look at a possible retirement scenario.

Mr. and Mrs. Jones are forced into early retirement at age 55. From a lump sum distribution of Mr. Jones's retirement plan plus other investment income, the Joneses have accumulated a retirement fund of $200,000.

According to life expectancy tables in Table 4-7 (these tables vary, depending on the source), Mr. Jones can look forward to almost 22 more years and his wife more than 25 years.

Mr. Jones finds a suitable investment paying 9 percent. Since this is not enough for their living expenses, each month they must withdraw part of their principal.

Table 4-6 shows that by withdrawing 10 percent from an investment earning 9 percent, the funds last 26 years. They can reasonably plan on monthly income of about $1,600 before taxes and about $1,400 after taxes.

There are many variables to influence how long money lasts. Inflation, health, family needs, and emergencies are only a few. This simple method, however, can help to plan for the future without too many surprises along the way.

Table 4-6
How Long Will Your Money Last?

Percentage of Original Principal Withdrawn per Year	Total Return per Year on Balance of Principal								
	6%	7%	8%	9%	10%	11%	12%	13%	14%
	The Number of Years Your Principal Will Last								
7%	33								
8%	23	30							
9%	18	22	28						
10%	15	17	20	26					
11%	13	14	16	19	25				
12%	11	12	14	15	18	23			
13%	10	11	12	13	15	17	22		
14%	9	10	10	11	13	14	17	21	
15%	8	9	9	10	11	12	14	16	20

Source: Edward D. Jones & Co.

Table 4-7
Life Expectancy Tables

Present Age	Life Expectancy No. of Years		Present Age	Life Expectancy No. of Years	
	Males	**Females**		**Males**	**Females**
45	29.6	33.8	61	17.5	21.0
46	28.7	33.0	62	16.9	20.3
47	27.9	32.1	63	16.2	19.6
48	27.1	31.2	64	15.6	18.9
49	26.3	30.4	65	15.0	18.2
50	25.5	29.6	66	14.4	17.5
51	24.7	28.7	67	13.8	16.9
52	24.0	27.9	68	13.2	16.2
53	23.2	27.1	69	12.6	15.6
54	22.4	26.3	70	12.1	15.0
55	21.7	25.5	71	11.6	14.4
56	21.0	24.7	72	11.0	13.9
57	20.3	24.0	73	10.5	13.2
58	19.6	23.2	74	10.1	12.6
59	18.9	22.4	75	9.6	12.1
60	18.2	21.7			

Source: U.S. Internal Revenue Life Expectancy Tables

Chapter 5

Special Funds for Special Purposes: or, Aren't They All Alike?

Each of us has the choice—we must make money
work for us, or we must work for money.
—*Conrad Leslie*

Every mutual fund has a specific investment objective
described in its prospectus. That objective also indicates
the amount of risk the fund owner can reasonably expect.
The fund's investment objective clearly states what you
should expect the fund to do—provide income, growth,
tax-free income, and more. Mutual funds are designed
for different investment purposes. They are not all alike.

At one time selecting a mutual fund was a relatively
simple matter. Today there are a multitude of different
mutual funds competing for your investment dollars. In
fact, mutual funds outnumber the securities listed on the
New York Stock Exchange.

While mutual funds are very popular now, most of
their growth has taken place during the last decade.
According to the Investment Company Institute, the
number of funds has increased roughly fivefold in the
past 10 years from 564 funds in 1980 to nearly 3,000
today (Appendix 1). And the number is still growing.

Mutual funds are probably the most popular way for small investors to pool their money and become part of large institutional-type accounts. Mutual funds aren't get-rich-quick schemes but rather long-range investment plans.

Those who have patience with well-selected mutual funds have seen their assets grow through the years. It's not uncommon to see conservative growth and income mutual funds compound at an average of more than 10 percent a year over a period of 15, 20, or 30 or more years. (Table 5-1)

Today's investors, however, are forcing a new challenge on the mutual fund industry—a challenge the industry may have brought on itself. The cry is for short-term performance. Some funds have successfully answered it. But keep in mind that the stock market doesn't go up forever.

Forbes recently pointed out that the average age of portfolio managers of one giant mutual fund group is 36. Several of their *sector funds*, those investing only in a specific industry, are managed by recent master's degree graduates as young as 26.

This doesn't suggest one must be older to wisely pick stocks. But an important part of managing money is not only picking stocks and making profits in a good market but also protecting both assets and profits in a bad market. Some of today's mutual fund managers have never experienced a bad market.

If this argument appears overconservative, and you're comfortable in the fast lane with a new generation of money managers, you've got a lot of company and a lot of funds from which to choose.

While it's fair to say that mutual funds can be many things to many people, it is equally unfair to say a single mutual fund can be all things to all people.

Today, with more than 3,000 different mutual funds offered to the public, there's one or more for your needs,

Table 5-1
Compounding Annual Rate of Return
Periods Ending December 31, 1989

15 Years (1975–1989)
(53 Funds)

Funds recording 12% or better comp ann rate of return	53
Funds recording 10% or better comp ann rate of return	53
Combined percent of total funds reporting (53)	100
Dow Junes Industrial Average	+ 15.8
S&P 500 Stock Index	+ 16.3
Cost of Living	+ 6.1
Johnson Growth & Income Fund Average	+ 16.5

20 Years (1970–1989)
(43 Funds)

Funds recording 12% or better comp ann rate of return	16
Funds recording 10% or better comp ann rate of return	17
Combined percent of total funds reporting (53)	76.7
Dow Junes Industrial Average	+ 11.3
S&P 500 Stock Index	+ 11.3
Cost of Living	+ 6.2
Johnson Growth & Income Fund Average	+ 11.7

30 Years (1960–1989)
(32 Funds)

Funds recording 12% or better comp ann rate of return	4
Funds recording 10% or better comp ann rate of return	13
Combined percent of total funds reporting (53)	53.1
Dow Junes Industrial Average	+ 9.1
S&P 500 Stock Index	+ 10.1
Cost of Living	+ 5.0
Johnson Growth & Income Fund Average	+ 10.3

Figures indicate total returns with all income and capital distributions reinvested in shares. All expenses and acquisition costs have been deducted.

Source: Johnson's Charts.

goals, and risk tolerance. The challenge is to find that fund before you invest.

The 1990 ICI *Guide to Mutual Funds* lists 22 different categories of mutual funds. Actually, these can be simplified into six *basic* fund types. Although each category offers a kaleidoscope of variations, most mutual funds are

1. income funds
2. growth and income funds
3. growth funds
4. balanced funds
5. sector funds
6. money market funds

What's an Income Fund?

The objective of *income funds* is to produce safe, regular income for the investor. To do this, fund managers generally invest in bonds or high-yielding preferred stocks.

Many retired people who enjoyed the benefit of a fund's growth during their working years may now find a 5 percent or 6 percent dividend little better than a savings account. They now need more income, more safety, and less growth. Many excellent mutual funds offer this.

An income fund is a reasonable answer to part of your retirement needs. Some offer current income of 10 percent or more. On a $100,000 investment this could mean enjoying a monthly check of over $800, rather than $500 or less offered by some growth funds. In addition, there is still the comfort of knowing that the investment is fully managed by professionals. Many look to income-oriented mutual funds for more spendable dollars.

Here again, a word of caution. A mutual fund dealing in senior securities (bonds) and paying a high current income is not an open passport to safety and security.

The key, as with all mutual funds, is management integrity and consistency. You find this only by research. With the help of a trained investment professional, look at a fund's record. There are several independent companies specializing in mutual fund research. These were discussed in Chapter 4. Compare the fund's results to other mutual funds with the same investment objectives. See how the fund's managers have done in the past year, five years, and longer. The information is available, but you have to make the effort to find it and study it.

All investments have some risk. The more risk, the more the borrower must pay the investor to take that risk. Some funds get very high income by investing in securities of lesser, questionable quality. Even though a fund is restricted only to senior securities, this doesn't eliminate risk. Higher income is often explained by more risk. The managers sacrifice some safety for more income.

If your income is needed for daily living expenses, it's important that the income be dependable. Regardless of the income promised today, it's of little value if reduced or stopped tomorrow.

Taxes are always a consideration. Regardless of whether you choose to receive your income in cash or have it reinvested, these distributions are taxed in the year declared. So you may consider avoiding all federal taxes on your mutual fund income. I realize this little scheme landed Al Capone in the slammer, so I appreciate your concern...

Can I Avoid Paying Taxes on Mutual Fund Income?

There's a special group of income funds that provide a good income exempt from federal taxes. These funds invest in tax-exempt securities of state, municipal, and public authority bonds. It's important to note that the income from these *tax-exempt funds* may be subject to state and local taxes. Discuss this with your tax consultant so you don't stub your toe and wind up in the county or state lockup. The biggest tax, however, is to the federal government, and income from tax-exempt mutual funds is exempt from federal tax.

There are several reasons to buy a tax-exempt mutual fund rather than an individual bond. The most important one to most investors is that your tax-exempt mutual fund is professionally managed. Traditionally tax-free municipals have been considered the highest-quality bonds after U.S. government issues. Although municipals still maintain this confidence for income and safety, no one should assume they're risk-free. According to a Green Financial Communications news release, 65 percent of the changes made in municipal bond ratings in 1988 by Standard & Poor's were downgrades. The issues were judged to be less creditworthy than previously.

This is not to suggest that municipals have become risky investments. They are still considered one of the safest ways to earn tax-free income. The safety of any investment, however, should not be taken for granted. During good economic times most reasonable investments do well, but as the economy slows, many previously attractive issues become vulnerable. By the time major rating services such as Moody's or Standard & Poor's downgrade an issue, it has probably already lost much of its value.

As monitoring individual bond issues becomes more difficult, many investors look to insured municipal bonds, bond trusts, or tax-free mutual bond funds.

Most tax-free mutual bond funds are not insured, but they are closely managed. Typically fund managers are in direct contact with the bond issuer. These managers look for financial stability and ask about future plans.

This can be an important asset. For instance, when a report described a questionable hospital bond a fund owned, one of the fund's analysts personally visited the facility and discovered some serious weaknesses at the hospital. The hospital's location had deteriorated, causing the beginning of a declining patient trend. Additionally, competition from adjoining hospitals suggested increasing revenue problems.

Before this became widely known, the fund was able to sell the bonds at no loss to its shareholders. Several months later these bonds went into technical default and lost 40 percent of their value. This example is not an isolated instance. Out of 180 municipal bond issues owned by this fund, only one was downgraded in 1988. Eighteen were upgraded.

The chief investment officer for the fund claimed no magical powers. Instead, he credited his success to personal visits and investigations which yielded information not made apparent solely by studying interest rate tables or annual reports. At a time when vigilance is becoming increasingly important, professional management for a part of your money deserves a serious look.

Another reason is that most tax-free bonds are printed in certificates of $5,000. This is the smallest investment you can make. Most mutual funds accept investments of $1,000 or less.

In addition, the fund can reinvest the income to compound tax-free. This benefit is not available with individual tax-free bonds.

You generally sacrifice a little current income from a fund as compared with a long-term (20—30 years) tax-exempt bond. The reason is that bonds bought for a mutual fund vary in maturity from very short, paying the least income, to very long, paying the most income. In this way there are bonds maturing regularly in the portfolio. When a bond matures, this money, along with new money invested, is used to buy more bonds at current rates. Your advantage is a flexible income. As interest rates change, you can benefit from these changes.

Avoid selecting a tax-exempt mutual fund only on the basis of current income. Read the prospectus. Learn the quality of bonds that the fund owns. You'll find this in the report to shareholders. It should be available through the representative offering the fund. Examine the rating of the bonds in the portfolio. Remember, the more risk in a bond, the more income it pays. The highest income usually means the highest risk.

Taxes may not be your main concern. If your aim is to get more income, even though it is taxable, please meet Ginnie Mae.

What's a Ginnie Mae Fund?

There is a group of mutual funds that has gained popularity in the past few years. These funds invest in securities issued or guaranteed by the U.S. government or its agencies. The funds are income-oriented, so the investments include bonds, notes, or U.S. Treasury bills.

Some investors, unsure of stock and corporate bonds, find comfort in securities backed by the full faith and credit of the U.S. government. Investing in government securities, however, generally requires more money. With limited funds, you're at a disadvantage in the large, complex government market. To meet the need for professional representation in the government market, mutual funds that invest only in U.S. government-guaranteed, or backed, securities were created. These securities include U.S. Government bonds, Government National Mortgage Association certificates (GNMAs, or Ginnie Maes), and other government and agency instruments.

Mutual funds restricted to these securities offer a fully managed portfolio of government securities. The benefit is regular interest payments, generally affected only by changes in interest rates. Some government-securities funds offer monthly checks not available through an individual investment.

Most government funds invest in government-backed home mortgages to *Ginnie Maes*. Some of the highest government interest is found in the mortgage market. It's a market dominated by specialists and institutional buyers. The expertise of the fund's managers and traders is there for shareholders of government-securities funds. These government funds offer benefits of small investments, monthly checks, and shares that can be redeemed at market value on any business day.

These funds made up of government securities offer another way to invest (IRA) funds. Most funds reinvest interest and earnings at no cost. Under an IRA, interest and earnings compound tax-sheltered until retirement. The added assurance is that these retirement funds are invested in securities protected or guaranteed by the U.S. government.

Thousands have placed part of their savings in mutual funds investing in Ginnie Maes. First mortgages on homes are considered among the most desirable income investments. Mortgage borrowers generally repay their debt promptly and regularly because the collateral pledged against the loan is their home. Any delinquency could result in eviction and loss of property. Add to this the protection offered by GNMA. In the event of any default, the U.S. government pays.

Since mutual funds continually issue new shares and redeem outstanding shares, this regular flow of cash requires that the funds invest in many Ginnie Mae pools of mortgages. Each pool has a different maturity and interest rate.

While the government does guarantee interest and principal on Ginnie Mae securities, it does not guarantee the future market value or the yield of the fund. Therefore, when investing in a Ginnie Mae fund, you must understand that although both principal and interest in the underlying securities is guaranteed, the yield and market value of your fund can and generally does fluctuate.

Most investments offer the same market fluctuation. For example, buy a small duplex to provide regular rent income. The good news is that during a period of rising prices, the value of the property could increase. In addition, the demand for housing could merit more rent. The bad news is that during a period of falling prices, the market value of the duplex could erode, and your rent could decline.

Every coin has two sides. But if you were assured that your rent would be comparable to other rent, that your duplex would be valued comparable to other duplexes, and that you could sell it at fair market value whenever necessary, this would eliminate some concern. That guarantee does not exist in real estate. But despite very few real estate guarantees, thousands of investors prudently assume the risks of real estate in hope of the rewards.

Compare the same illustration with a Ginnie Mae mutual fund with an average income yield of about 9 percent. On a $100,000 investment you would expect a $750 check each month. Keep in mind, this is paid from interest earned on the GNMA mortgages held by the fund. If interest on home mortgages declines and new GNMAs are offering only 7 percent, the portfolio's average yield will also decline because of dilution by lower-interest GNMAs. Your monthly checks will be slightly less—but comparable to and generally more than you could receive with other investments of similar quality. Your mutual fund interest fluctuates because of interest rate changes.

The same fluctuation occurs in most income investments. A certificate of deposit earning 6 percent might earn only 5 percent when you renew it next year. It could also earn 7 percent. It fluctuates. With Ginnie Mae mutual funds the fluctuations are slower and less dramatic.

Another feature of a Ginnie Mae mutual fund that could be confusing is the daily market value of the fund shares. Since Ginnie Maes are guaranteed by the U.S. government, doesn't that mean you can withdraw all your investments at any time without loss? Yes, you can withdraw your investment at any time, but at current market value. That value could be more, the same, or less than your deposit. A little understanding of Ginnie Maes tells why.

Ginnie Mae mutual funds should be long-term investments. They can't be compared to bank savings or certificates of deposit that generally earn less interest but offer immediate liquidation—although often with withdrawal penalties.

Investing in Ginnie Mae funds should be viewed as buying rental property. Your money works for you earning regular monthly income, usually more than you could earn on a savings account or certificate of deposit. Ginnie Maes are pools of long-term mortgages, so they should not be bought as short-term investments. Since the interest on most mortgages remains constant, the market value must fluctuate along with current interest rates.

For example, invest $10,000 at 12 percent, and earn a steady $1,200 annually. If rates drop to 9 percent, a similar $10,000 investment now earns $900, and your investment, earning more income, becomes more valuable. But if rates move up to 14 percent, a new $10,000 investment would earn $1,400. Your investment would now be less valuable.

Since a fund's portfolio is made up of hundreds of mortgages paying different rates of interest, you see that the market value of the fund changes slightly as interest rates change. In a mutual fund it's not as dramatic as our example, since new money is constantly being added to a Ginnie Mae fund and invested at current rates.

A second way the market value of your fund could be affected is by prepayment of the mortgages held by the fund. For example, if a fund owns some 12 percent mortgages and new mortgages are 10 percent, the higher-yielding mortgages would have a *premium* market value. This premium is reflected in the overall value of the fund. But if that 12 percent mortgage is prepaid by the borrower, it is generally prepaid at face value. The premium disappears, and the value of the fund is reduced by that premium. Of course, that would not dramatically affect you unless you bought into the fund when the value of its shares included a large premium price.

This sounds more confusing than it is. The important thing is, before investing in Ginnie Mae mutual funds, to ask and understand the record of past interest payments and whether the value of the shares reflects an unreasonable premium. Your broker should be able to explain this. If not, look for another broker or another fund.

Although Ginnie Maes are guaranteed by the U.S. government, the interest and value of your mutual fund shares are subject to market fluctuations. For safe, reliable income, Ginnie Mae mutual funds can be excellent investments. But understand them before you invest. Income investing should also meet your safety needs.

Ask about risk and get answers. Income has gained as an investor objective. In 1983 bond and income funds accounted for 14 percent of total mutual fund assets. By 1989 that figure had more than doubled to 31 percent (Appendix 2).

What's a Growth and Income Fund?

Another basic type of mutual fund is a *long-term growth with current income secondary fund*. Remember, *long-term means more than five years.*

A mutual fund with a long-term growth objective looks for investments that have not yet reached full potential. These usually have a proven record of performance in their industry, but unlike established companies, these younger, growth-oriented firms dedicate a major portion of earnings to expansion. So they pay little or no dividends. Mutual funds select these companies to benefit from present growth and participate in future income as it is paid.

No one knows what the cost of living will be in five years. Most agree it will be more. To meet rising prices, you must plan for a rising income. Investors need to see income checks grow. Bonds and other fixed-income investments don't offer a growing income, but many growth and income mutual funds do.

I looked at the 50th annual report of a mutual fund whose objective is long-term growth of capital, with more emphasis on *future* rather than on *current* income. In other words, they buy stocks to grow and increase dividends along with inflation.

Based on a $10,000 investment, the first dividend, in 1936, was $387. That was just under 4 percent. From there the income doubled on an average of every eight years. In 1940 the fund paid $782; by 1947 it had risen to $1,624; in 1959, $3,070; 1967, $6,669; 1974, $15,445; and in 1987 the fund paid $46,069 in income. That's over four times the original $10,000 investment. In the meantime, the original investment had grown to $1,185,370. This fund was not selected as an example because of exceptional income performance. The principle of studying the history of growing income—or lack of it—works with any mutual fund. If you are interested in more income through the years, examine the fund's past ability to increase income; the annual report is an excellent and easily accessible place to start.

There are no guarantees, but consistent results is a useful yardstick when selecting a growth and income mutual fund.

When Should I Invest in a Growth Fund?

So far we've talked about mutual funds that pay current income. Some people like and want the possibility of growth. On the other hand, growth generally offers little or no current income. When you buy a mutual fund hoping to sell it at a profit sometime later, you are a growth investor. Uncertainty, the risk of waiting, coupled with little or no income during this time makes growth mutual funds unsuited for some investors.

Before making any investment, it's a good policy to decide what you're *not* going to invest in. If you dislike Chinese food, why spend a lot of time evaluating Chinese restaurants? If for some reason growth investments don't fit into your plans, why spend a lot of time with them? It makes sense to set them aside and concentrate on immediate needs. Circumstances may alter your decision, but for the time being concentrate on what you need now.

If you need a steady income to meet living expenses, you should consider something other than growth mutual funds. Growth investments generally reinvest profits for expansion, new equipment, building, and the like. That leaves little to be paid in dividends to shareholders. This is how companies grow. Growth mutual funds invest in these stocks. But a lot of future hope doesn't pay today's rent. If current income is your need, growth is not your answer. Consider more suitable investments.

I often hear the boast, "I like to gamble." More honestly it should be, "I like to win." Even the best-researched investments can't guarantee a winner. Investing is not an exact science. The more risk you add to it, the less the chances of winning. The sophisticated investor knows that mutual fund values fluctuate, and growth investments are for the long pull. If risk is not for you, growth investments can add a lot of stress to your life.

If on the other hand, you decide some growth is needed in your investment plan, seriously consider...

What Can a Growth Fund Do for Me?

Growth investments have proved well suited for those who want to build an estate. For example, you've raised your family, and the expenses of children and education are behind. Your current income gives a comfortable living, some luxuries, and enough left for investing. A growth investment could offer some advantages. Retirement is 15 to 20 years away. With a regular investment program, in 20 years a modest monthly deposit in a growth-oriented mutual fund could produce a respectable nest egg for those retirement years.

In a real-life example one group of professional money managers in a recent 20-year period (1968—1987) managed to produce for their investors a nest egg of $104,834. (See Table 5-2.) What did the investors do? They initially deposited $250 and added $100 per month for the next 20 years. Of course, they didn't expect their investment to perform the same each year. Some years were better than others. They were concerned, however, with long-term results. They examined the management results since 1934, when the mutual fund began. In the best 20-year period (1949—1968), the managers built a modest $100 per month into over $128,000. In the worst period (1955—1974), it grew to over $45,000.

In these examples all capital gains and income were reinvested to compound. The goal was to accumulate a nest egg for retirement. If the fund you are considering does not publish a similar long-term accumulation record, ask for one. Most funds are happy to offer hypothetical illustrations like this.

Assume the same investor chose instead of growth to take the same $100 per month for the same 20 years and place it in a more secure investment that averaged 6 percent annually. If nothing were withdrawn, it would have compounded to just about $47,000, about the same as the worst 20-year period with the growth investment.

Once you decide your risk tolerance, you are in a better position to decide if growth mutual funds are for you. Many investors find them one way to build for retirement.

Table 5-2
If You're Interested in Investing Monthly
Here's what would have happened if you had invested $250 and added $100 every month for 20 years (total investment $24,150). Here's how you would have done in every 20-year period in the Fund's history.

Jan.1–Dec/ 31	Dividends Reinvested	Total Cost (including dividends)	Capital Gains Taken in Shares	Ending Value of Shares
1934–1953	$20,706	$44,856	$22,138	$ 76,013
1935– 1954	19,967	44,117	23,135	103,655
1936–1955	19,636	43,786	27,076	113,633
1937–1956	20,633	44,683	32,583	116,063
1938–1957	22,022	46,172	36,168	98,643
1939–1958	21,860	46,010	35,720	124,766
1940–1959	21,782	45,932	39,722	128,003
1941–1960	21,555	46,705	40,827	118,964
1942–1961	20,772	44,922	41,451	128,247
1943–1962	19,302	43,452	38,380	94,830
1944–1963	18,394	42,544	36,623	1 1,930
1945–1964	17,742	41,892	37,189	,662
1946–1965	17,455	41,605	39,302	118,699
1947–1966	17,924	42,074	43,0	109,020
1948–1967	18,047	42,197	43,1	124,915
1949–1968	18,207	42,357	41,487	128,493
1950–1969	17,814	41,964	41,043	9 ,660
1951–1970	17,257	41,407	37,648	, 83
1952–1971	16,780	40,930	33,092	8,825
1953–1972	16,068	40,218	30,01	89,825
1954"1973	15,153	39,303	25,	63,764
1955–1974	15,176	39,326	20,983	45,341
1956–1975	15,385	39,536	17,956	56,258
1957–1976	15,387	39,517	16,215	64,995
1958–1977	15,187	39,337	14,756	57,236
1959–1978	14,728	38,876	11,993	58,273
1960–1979	15,037	39,187	10,666	63,356
1961–1980	16,623	39,773	10,159	69,600
1962–1981	16,689	40,839	12,780	64,046
1963–1982	17,848	41,998	14,328	, 24
1964–1983	18,376	42,626	14,944	,046
1965–1984	19,061	43,201	16,088	80,211
1966–1985	19,707	43,867	17,0	97,149
1967–1986	20,785	44,936	32,08	108,402
1968–1987	22,448	46,598	34,497	104,834

BEST PERIOD *WORST PERIOD* *LATEST PERIOD*

This example is for illustrative purposes only and does not imply future results.

Why Can't I Just Invest in the Winners?

There's no better way to see how following winners can make you a loser than by looking at what happens to last year's top fund.

Most serious investing is done for the future. Erratic spurts of genius generally are not as important as long-term results. Yet some are still tempted to look at the hot performers—THE NUMBER ONE FUND OF THE YEAR.

Jim Weddle, a mutual fund specialist with a major New York Stock Exchange member firm, gathered some eye-opening information on investing in the best-performing fund of the previous year. What would happen if you carefully followed more than 2,000 mutual funds and each year invested in the top-performing fund of the previous year? After all, since one can't predict the future, going with the best fund now seems to make sense.

On January 1, 1975, Weddle hypothetically invested $10,000 in the best-performing fund of 1974. On January 1 of each of the next 12 years, he moved the investment to the best-performing fund of the previous year. All dividends and capital gains were reinvested, and all purchases were made without a sales charge. Table 5-3 shows a year-by-year value that would have accumulated by switching to each year's number one account. As you see, by always following the previous year's top fund, by December 31, 1987, $10,000 grew into $52,680—not a bad return on your investment.

What if you had made a one-time $10,000 investment on January 1, 1975, and let it compound undisturbed for the same 12-year period? As Table 5-4 shows, Fund A grew to $76,757, Fund B to $70,519, and Fund C to $68,602. All outperformed the investor who chose to follow last year's hottest number.

An important thing to understand about this illustration is that none of the funds Weddle selected were ever recognized as the year's top-performing fund. In fact, they seldom if ever made the top-performance lists of

Table 5-3
Investing in Previous Year's Top Fund

Year	#1 Fund's % Return	Next Year	#1 Fund's Next Year % Return	$10,000 Now Worth
1974	10.9	1974	−24.1	$ 7,590
1975	184.1	1973	46.5	11,119
1976	72.5	1975	19.9	13,332
1977	51.5	1976	27.6	17,012
1978	58.9	1977	−23.4	13,031
1979	187.3	1978	78.9	23,312
1980	93.9	1979	−13.2	20,235
1981	48.2	1980	81.3	36,686
1982	81.3	1981	24.8	45,785
1983	68.1	1982	−28.0	32,965
1984	48.6	1983	26.5	41,701
1985	69.6	1984	11.4	46,455
1986	77.8	1985	13.4	52,680

Table 5-4
Consistent Investment in Same Fund
Value of $10,000 Invested

Year	Fund A	Fund B	Fund C
1975	$12,388	$13,002	$11,863
1976	15,066	17,459	14,627
1977	15,641	16,245	14,689
1978	17,940	16,766	16,567
1979	21,379	21,611	20,245
1980	25,618	26,840	27,768
1981	26,146	26,829	26,977
1982	34,976	33,122	33,030
1983	42,029	41,453	40,267
1984	44,382	44,135	42,437
1985	59,802	55,843	54,518
1986	72,799	68,502	66,974
1987	76,757	70,519	68,602

This example is for illustrative purposes only and does not imply further results.

financial publications that annually rate mutual funds. The secret of their success was to aim for reasonable investment results, total return, or a combination of growth and income and do it consistently.

The table shows that consistent results with no devastating surprises puts you well ahead over the long haul—up to 46 percent ahead in the case of Fund A.

Investing offers few guarantees, but experience shows that money managers who aim for consistent, reasonable results by investing in quality securities generally outperform both the overall market and the speculator chasing the hottest fund around.

What's a Balanced Fund? Balanced funds are among the most conservative funds you can own. As their name suggests, they are "balanced" between stocks and bonds.

At one time the balance, or proportion, the portfolio manager was allowed to place in either stocks or bonds was excessively restrictive. For example, if the prospectus limited the fund's assets to a maximum of 60 percent in equities, then regardless of how good the equity market or how bad the bond market, the portfolio manager could not exceed the fund's allowed limits.

Today most funds are more liberal with their balance demands. At times their portfolio could have a mix of securities that closely resembles a growth and income fund.

Generally, however, a balanced fund keeps 20 to 40 percent of assets in bonds or preferred stocks. The common stock of well-capitalized, established companies makes up most of the remaining portfolio. You can examine this mix, or balance, by referring to the fund's latest quarterly or annual report.

It is particularly important before investing in a balanced fund to read the prospectus.

Since balanced funds appeal more to the conservative investor, it is necessary to decide how conservative the fund is.

Some funds still define the limits of bond or equity investments in the portfolio at any one time. Others are more general and allow the portfolio manager a wider latitude in selection.

For example, one balanced fund describes their investments as being like "the complete investment program of the prudent investor." That means they must diversify and balance their portfolio. It does not, however, place limitations or define the extent of the diversification.

They go on to say that this is a "carefully selected, supervised and broadly diversified list of securities, including common stocks, preferred stocks, and corporate and government bonds...considered advisable by the investment adviser."

Although the objectives and limitations are often general, they are in no way misleading. To see how successfully they accomplish these objectives, you must examine the fund's historical performance. Remember, balanced funds tend to underperform all-equity or stock funds in good markets and offer an edge of market protection in bad markets.

How Can You Judge
a Balanced Fund's Success?

To illustrate a technique I use, compare the five-year and ten-year performance of one balanced fund to a quality growth and income fund managed by the same fund group (figure 5-1).

As you see, the growth and income fund did outperform the balanced fund over meaningful periods of both five and ten years. However, during 1987, which included the severe market decline of October, the balanced fund offered a bit more downside protection.

It is also important to note that this balanced fund, over this ten-year period, with an average annual com-

---

Figure 5-1

Annual Compounded Rate of Return
(January 1, 1978 through December 31, 1987 with
all distributions reinvested)

Balanced Fund A		**Growth Income Fund B**
+12.41%	Latest 10 Yrs	+16.35%
+12.76%	Latest 5 Yrs	+15.50%
– 4.85%	Latest 1 Yr	– 7.20%

---

pounded rate of return of 12.4 percent, *underperformed* the S&P 500 (15.2 percent) and the Dow Jones Industrials (14.6 percent). Both indexes are made up of common stock equities.

On the other hand, this balanced fund *outperformed* the Salomon Brothers High-Grade Corporate Bond Index (9.7 percent) and the average yearly increase in the cost of living as measured by the Consumer Price Index (6.4 percent).

The purpose of this exercise is to offer a simple technique to evaluate a balanced fund. Here is a simple checklist I suggest. A balanced fund

1. should underperform comparable growth and income funds in good markets (if it outperforms them, great!);
2. should offer downside protection in bad markets;
3. should offer a better total return than high-grade corporate bonds; and
4. should keep you ahead of inflation by out- performing the CPI.

If you are a conservative investor who still wants some opportunity of growth to hedge against inflation, balanced funds deserve your consideration.

What's a Sector Fund?

About 10 years ago it appeared we were headed for unprecedented, worldwide oil shortages. The price of oil was skyrocketing. Some predicted oil at $100 a barrel and said that coal would be the major fuel source for electric power. In short, we faced a long and severe oil crisis.

Although many analysts warned the investment community that the oil patch hadn't dried up, there was still enough smoke in the air to suggest a little fire. Add to that the chance for a quick buck—getting in on the ground floor, so to speak—and you have the perfect scenario for a new sector fund.

Energy stocks were making new highs, so no one was buying bargains. But everyone "knew" this was the beginning. Energy stocks "had" to go higher.

Although my conservative philosophy warned, "wait and see," the euphoria of the times prompted me to take a chance. Since I decided to commit only a small investment to energy stocks, a well-chosen sector fund seemed reasonable. After reading the prospectuses of several energy funds, I made an investment in a newly issued fund with a reasonably sound portfolio of energy stocks.

The investment philosophy of the fund was somewhat aggressive but managed within the parameters of the prospectus. By the following year, however, my original investment had lost a large part of its value.

Owning part of the economy through selective mutual funds is not without risk. My loss, however, was unreasonable. It was not necessarily the fault of the fund's management but rather violation of my own investment principles.

A major benefit of owning a mutual fund is spreading risk through diversification. In most cases this means not only diversification of securities but also diversification of industries (Appendix 3). Sector funds, however, confine their investments to stocks of companies within a specific industry. The good news is, if the industry does well, the sector fund can shine. The bad news is, if the industry does poorly, the sector fund is generally hardest hit.

Shortly after making my original investment, U.S. dependence on foreign oil was reevaluated. Suddenly the entire industry was taking on a new investment flavor. Energy stocks across the board declined. My sector fund suffered.

Another error was evaluating management in terms of expertise in one industry rather than an overall proven record of money management. Overspecialized experts often suffer tunnel vision—the "this-can't-be-happening" philosophy. Even when they recognize industry deterioration, they have no place else to go.

My purpose is not to discourage investing a *part* of your assets in a specific industry through a sector fund. It is rather to illustrate how an untimely decision can result in a major investment setback. The illustration fund has since regained that initial loss and yielded a very modest positive total return over the years. But it has not, in my opinion, been an overall good investment.

On the positive side, sector funds offer the opportunity to participate in numerous exciting industries, such as communications, electronics, health care, aerospace, precious metals, natural resources, options, foreign investments, utilities, and more. One sector group that has continued to keep investors' interest is utilities. Utilities are always in vogue because they are a necessary, rather than a fad, industry. This does not say that the industry has not experienced bad times. But utility stocks generally pay good dividends. They are relatively stable, because of regulation and protection within the industry. Utilities are not without risk, but conservative investors tend to find some security in utility stocks because of the overall total return. Utility sector funds offer such an investor the opportunity to diversify risk in this industry and still enjoy the benefits of professional mutual fund management.

Not all sector funds are so clear-cut in objectives or predictable in results. Sector funds require more study and understanding than most mutual funds. If your selected sector fund has an investment record, compare that record to the entire industry.

Many industries are cyclical. They may benefit strongly from favorable economic conditions and suffer hardest from a weak economy.

Others get a temporary boost from fads. Again, I recall during the oil crisis how some prophets of doom predicted the gasoline engine would soon be obsolete. Diesels and rotaries were the future. If some enterprising money manager could have found enough stock in this isolated industry, probably a specialized sector fund could have lured enough investors to make it interesting. Unless you closely monitor your fund, your investment could still be parked when the fad is gone.

There is a special category of mutual funds that can probably be classified as a type of sector fund. These funds are designed for investors with very strict religious or social convictions. You might even ask...

What Do Personal Moral Convictions Have to Do with Investing?

Several years ago I suggested a portfolio of high-yielding, blue-chip securities to a client. The purpose of the investment was to give a generous income and reasonable safety while still offering some opportunity of growth. One company whose stock was included in the proposed portfolio offered tobacco as part of its product line.

My client emphatically rejected any company that sold or promoted tobacco. While I viewed the stock only from an investment value, my client saw its social or religious significance.

Many people, because of strict religious or social convictions, refuse to invest in companies whose business violates their principles. Their wishes must be respected.

When selecting individual securities, this seldom presents a problem. A little research generally uncovers a company's complete product line. If you can't get full satisfaction from Moody's, Standard & Poor's, or Value Line, a note to the company's headquarters generally brings a handsome and informative annual report. Not only will you see an array of present products, but most companies are quick to outline future plans, products, and prospects.

If these do not correspond with or, worse, violate your convictions, don't invest. That's simple enough, but what if you are investing in mutual funds?

Today mutual funds invest not only for the small, individual investor but also for major retirement plans, endowment funds, trusts, colleges, and more. One mutual fund recently reported that they "manage money for more than 8,000 institutional investors—over $740 million in all, including about $425 million for retirement plan accounts." And this is only one mutual fund. Of course, if your retirement dollars are part of your company's multimillion-dollar plan, you probably have little or no say as to how those funds are invested.

If you select a mutual fund, you are placing your confidences in the managers of that fund and, in fact, giving them total discretion, within the limits set forth in the prospectus, as to where to invest your money. If they choose a stock that does not meet your approval, your choice is to accept it or to liquidate your fund shares.

A mutual fund's portfolio does not in actual practice get a lot of review or criticism from the shareholders. The fund's current holdings are listed in the annual and quarterly reports, sent to all shareholders. Beyond that there is little way to know what the managers are buying or selling.

Most mutual fund shareholders don't care as long as the results are good. If you are one of the select few who may be interested in the social or religious implications of your investments but still like the benefits of mutual fund investing, take heart. *Changing Times* magazine some time ago addressed the question of the *social funds*.

Changing Times reviewed five of these special-purpose funds, handling a large part of some $1 billion invested in this manner. No doubt the number will continue to grow if they are successful. A special report by *Insight*, an advisery letter published in Boston, lists nine of these "socially responsible funds" and two money market funds.

The funds range in size from a low of less than $5 million in assets with about 650 shareholders to a high of more than $180 million in assets with 13,000 shareholders. The oldest of these funds was started in 1971, so *Changing Times* finds it "tough to assay social funds in general against the fund universe—they're too new." They point out that only two "have existed through a complete cycle of up and down stock markets."

What these funds do invest in varies with the risk philosophy and policy of the funds. What they do not invest in is very similar—no alcohol, tobacco, nuclear power, or gambling.

One fund manager is quick to point out that they are not out to change the world, just invest responsibly. But what is responsible? Again, it boils down to a matter of individual conscience. Whereas some look on defense spending as immoral, one fund's largest holdings are in stocks of companies who deal in defense contracting. That's responsible only if you agree with their moral values.

If you haven't seen an abundance of advertising on these funds, it could be because they often direct those advertising dollars to publications that appeal to the largest segment of potential investors. For example, one fund whose investments are primarily environmental in scope promote their fund through the environmental publications.

If you are interested in knowing more about "socially acceptable" stocks, a call or letter to the Social Investment Forum, 711 Atlantic Avenue, Boston, MA 02111 (telephone: (617) 423-6655) will put you in contact with the right people.

What Are the Advantages of a Family of Funds?

No discussion of mutual funds is complete without mentioning the *family of funds.*

Most mutual fund groups manage several different funds with different investment objectives. This is their family of funds. It allows investors the opportunity to divide deposits among several funds and still enjoy the same overall management group. Investing in a family of funds versus a single individual fund also lets you switch into other funds within that family at little or no cost.

According to a 1986 ICI survey, 51 percent of mutual fund investors who buy shares direct select a particular mutual fund because of the family of funds to which it belongs (Appendix 4).

The concept of having the bulk of your mutual fund investment in a single group having a number of funds with different objectives makes sense. The key, however, is to select a group with a long record of consistent overall money management results.

Financial World, a respected financial publication, recently helped identify top mutual fund groups by doing some of the homework.

Financial World publishes ratings on about 1,050 relatively large mutual funds. According to publisher Douglas McIntyre, for this study they took all the families with six or more funds and averaged the rankings of their individual funds. For example, if Study Fund Number One had six rated funds that ranked 2, 180, 625, 480, 571, 720 out of the total 1,050 funds, these numbers totaled and divided by six equal 429.6.

McIntyre allowed a deviation of 50 ranking points from the 525 midpoint of his 1,050 funds for a fund family's performance to qualify as "mediocre"—475 to 575. "Good" families scored from 425 to 475. Lower than 475 was "extraordinary" performance for a fund family. A score of 575 to 625 was "poor"; greater than 625 was "unacceptable."

The results of the study showed that only six of 51 fund families rated as extraordinary (263.3—416.5). Six also rated as good (427.4—474.7). Sixteen were mediocre (477.1—571.5). Six were poor (575.3—619.0), and 17 were unacceptable (632.1—811.5).

McIntyre concluded that "the largest and most advertised mutual fund companies aren't necessarily the best."

The study offered one disadvantage for the average investor. It rated the performance of *all* the funds within a family. Most investors would not consider exchanging among 63 different funds. That's how many the largest group had. Next was 34, then downward to 6.

To make this personally meaningful, the comparison of only those mutual funds with investment objectives the same as yours should be included in your study. The purpose of the exercise is to select the mutual fund family with the best-performing individual funds within your objective and risk parameters. A little homework and a pocket calculator could make and save you precious investment dollars when selecting your mutual funds.

Why Avoid Lesser-Known Funds?

The overall performance of a mutual fund family should be a major concern, but it does not guarantee stellar or even acceptable performance from all its members.

Ever watch a child choose among 31 flavors of ice cream? Generally he settles for an old standard like vanilla or chocolate and walks away happy. Occasionally, however, one ventures into the unknown, chances something like a honey-licorice, and regrets it.

Investors face much the same challenge. Now and then a fund with an exciting name or unique twist lures us away from the tried and tested. And like the child with the curious taste buds, we often regret it.

It was this ice-cream-parlor philosophy that drew me to a recent *Changing Times* article (October 1990) on the mutual fund "hall of shame." The focus of this book is on the long-term benefits of carefully selected mutual funds. The key words are *long-term* and *carefully selected*. Accept less, and you could wind up in the mutual fund hall of shame. The hall is full of growth funds that don't grow, market-timers on the wrong time, and gold funds without their shine.

Changing Times is quick to point out that most of these awful records belong to small funds with a limited, or no, investment record. As performance declines (or never starts), no new money comes in. The fund's assets shrink along with its chance for recovery. Here is a sample of a few miserable records.

One "developing growth fund" grew 6 percent in five years. Keep in mind this was during a time when some similar funds were averaging gains of 120 percent and more over that same period. This loser did manage, however, to pay out more than $9 million in commissions to their sales force. Remember, the cost of running a mutual fund continues even if you aren't making money.

Here's another horror story. According to *Changing Times* this small company fund had "too much turnover, poor stock picking and sector ideas that didn't work." The fund is now a tax shelter that boasts of $1.6 million in tax losses carried forward. That means that shareholders won't be taxed on the next $1.6 million of capital gains distributed. What gains? The fund's total five-year return was only 3.9 percent.

Then there is the fund whose legendary 73 percent loss for the 1980s caused their assets to go from $245 million to $5 million. "In 1988 the Securities and Exchange Commission evicted the former boss and manager," says *Changing Times*. The charge: breaching his fiduciary duties. I'm sure this gave shareholders a warm feeling of justice, but it did little to soothe their losses.

There was a gold fund that missed every market cycle and lost 18.7 percent in five years; there was a special fund designed to follow corporate raiders, and while chasing them turned every dollar invested into 70 cents; and a fund that owned almost exclusively South African mining shares at such an inopportune time that it lost 43 percent of its value *after* the low point in the U.S. stock market (December 2, 1987).

These examples are not cited to scare you away from mutual funds. They simply illustrate the hazards of venturing sizable investments into unknown mutual funds. A *modest* taste of any of these funds would have meant a loss, but not a financial tragedy. When in doubt, try just a taste. You know what to expect from the old standards.

CHAPTER 6

MANAGING YOUR MUTUAL FUNDS: OR, AREN'T THEY MANAGED ALREADY?

According to the Investment Company Institute, total assets of all mutual funds in 1990 reached $1 trillion (Appendix 5). In 1988, at about 55 million, shareholder accounts had more than doubled since 1983 (Appendix 6). Many of these shareholders own mutual funds because they don't have the time or expertise to research stocks, buy them, and then decide when to sell. Instead they turn to proven professional money managers through the purchase of mutual funds.

Mutual funds offer the benefit of professional money management. That should not suggest that you select a fund, invest your money, and come back in 20 years expecting to be rich.

Even considering the excellent long-term performance of many mutual funds, you should regularly monitor your investments. Since mutual funds are designed for long-term investing, the daily fluctuation is not a major concern. However, a quarterly review of its progress—or lack of it—should be made. The simplest way to do this is read your shareholder's statement (Figure 6-1). After that you might ask...

What Is NAV?

Mutual funds must declare their net asset value (NAV) each day at the close of business. This is done by pricing each security in the portfolio, adding any cash and accrued earnings, subtracting liabilities, and dividing by the number of shares outstanding. For example, if the total value of a fund's portfolio is $10 million and there are 1 million shares outstanding, each share is worth $10. If you own 100 shares of the fund, the value of your investment is $1,000.

Mutual funds make payments to shareholders in dividends and capital gains. Although not required, most funds pay dividends quarterly [Figure 6-1(a)] and capital gains annually [Figure 6-1(b)]. In some cases more than one capital gain could be distributed in a year. If you are a shareholder of a mutual fund and the board of directors declares a dividend or capital gain, when it's paid, it's recorded on your statement [Figure 6-1(a and b)]. If you've chosen to receive this in cash, a check is mailed, and your statement will show the date and amount of that payment. If your payment is reinvested into additional shares of the fund, your statement will show the date [Figure 6-1(c)], quarterly dividend per share and dollar amount reinvested [Figure 6-1(d)], price per share [Figure 6-1(e)], how many shares purchased [Figure 6-1(f)], and new balance of shares [Figure 6-1(g)]. By reinvesting your dividends and capital gains, your shares increase in number through the years [Figure 6-1(h)]. This is compounding.

So to know how many shares you own at any time, refer to your last shareholder statement [Figure 6-1(i)]. Once you know your share number, go to your newspaper, look at the NAV of your fund for that day [Figure

Figure 6-1

MOST ANY GROWTH-INCOME FUND, INC.
INDIVIDUAL RETIREMENT ACCOUNT

ACCOUNT NUMBER
1234567-0

SOCIAL SECURITY ON
TAXPAYER IDENTIFICATION NO.
(REQUIRED BY LAW)
444-444-444

SALES REPRESENTATIVE
SERVICING YOUR ACCOUNT
JOE SALESMAN

DEALER NO. BRANCH
123-4567

STATEMENT DATE
12/05/86

JOE E DOKES &
MARY Z DOKES   TEN COM
100 PLAZA
ANYTOWN, USA

ACCOUNT OPTION
DIV-R   CAP-R

(d) AMOUNT DIV/CAP
GAIN PAID
PER SHARE

(e) PRICE PER SHARE
(f) NUMBER SHARES
PURCHASED

INDIVIDUAL TRANSACTIONS FOR YEAR TO DATE

CONFIRM DATE	TRADE DATE	TRANSACTION DESCRIPTION		DOLLAR AMOUNT	PRICE PER SHARE	SHARE THIS TRANSACTION	TOTAL SHARES OWNED
		BEGINNING BALANCE					5,339.87
2/12	2/05	INCOME DIVIDEND	.13	694.18	12.030	57.704	5,397.57
4/29	4/22	INCOME DIVIDEND	.13	701.69	11.850	59.214	5,456.79
4/29	4/22	CAPITAL GAIN	.24	1,295.42	11.850	109.318	5,566.11
8/08	8/05	INCOME DIVIDEND	.13	723.59	12.460	58.073	5,624.81
11/07	11/04	INCOME DIVIDEND	.13	731.14	12.630	57.889	5,682.67
12/19	12/16	INCOME DIVIDEND	.04	227.28	12.56	18.096	5,700.16

(a) DIVIDENDS PAID
(b) CAPITAL GAIN PAID
(c) TRADE DATE OF PAYMENT

(g) NEW SHARE BALANCE
(h) INCREASE IN SHARE BALANCE

(i) TOTAL SHARES OWNED

YEAR TO DATE ACCOUNT SUMMARY

INCOME DIVIDENDS INVESTED	CAPITAL GAINS REINVESTED	TOTAL SHARES OWNED
3077.88	1,295.42	5,700.169

This example is for illustrative purposes only and does not imply future results.

6-2(a)], and multiply by your number of shares: that's how much your investment is worth. For example, if you own 1,000 shares of a fund whose NAV is 14.58, your investment is worth $14,580.

What Do Those Numbers
in the Newspaper Mean?

A client recently asked how to determine the value of his mutual fund. I explained how to read the shareholder's statement and find his share balance.

"But how do I know how much each share is worth?" he asked. The answer is important to anyone who owns mutual funds.

If you subscribe to *The Wall Street Journal*, you have a comprehensive daily list of mutual fund quotations. If you're not a *Journal* subscriber, most major metropolitan newspapers carry a select listing of funds in the financial section. The funds are generally listed in standard format [Figure 6-2]. Major management groups appear alphabetically in bold print [Figure 6-2(b)]. Under the group follows a listing of all funds that are managed by that group. This is their family of funds. For example, if you own any of the American Funds Group, look down the column until you see that group [Figure 6-2(b)]. Directly below are 21 mutual funds that the American Group publicly manages. The names of the individual funds, although abbreviated, are easily recognized [Figure 6-2(c)].

Once you have located your fund, the number to the immediate right is the NAV [Figure 6-2(d)]. Since most mutual funds have no redemption charge, the NAV represents what you would receive for each share owned and redeemed on that particular day.

The next number is the offering price. This price is the NAV plus the maximum sales charge, if any [Figure

Figure 6-2

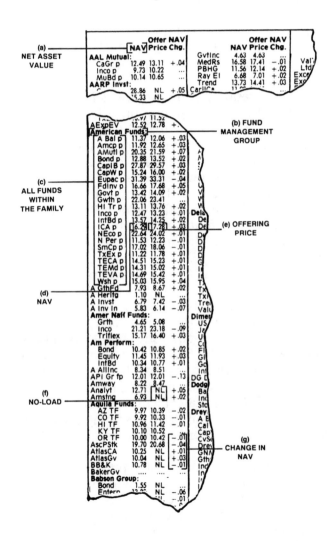

6-2(e)]. Funds offer a reduced sales charge based on the amount invested. The larger your investment, the smaller the sales charge. Funds vary, but that charge can range from high of 8.5 percent of the offering price to a low of 1 percent. So if your investment qualifies for the reduced charge, the amount you pay is less than the quoted offering price.

An "NL" beside the fund indicates there is no sales charge included in the offering price [Figure 6-2(f)]. It does not necessarily mean that the fund has no sales charge. The fund could have a back-end load, a charge for withdrawal, a contingent deferred sales charge, or a 12b-1 plan, which permits a special deduction for commission from the fund's assets. This is indicated by a "p," an "r," or a "t" [Figure 6-3(a)]. You only know this if you carefully study the fund's prospectus. Although "NL" symbolizes "no load," it is not a guarantee there are no sales charges.

The change in NAV is represented in cents and preceded by a plus or minus, indicating that the fund gained or lost in value that day [Figure 6-2(g)]. If there is an unusually large drop in the fund's value, it may be due to a dividend or capital gain distribution. This means the fund shares are valued at "ex" or without dividend [Figure 6-3(c)]. They may select to use "xd" instead, which means the same thing. For example, if a fund pays a 50-cent dividend, the NAV decreases by that amount. An "f" next to your fund simply means that, due to the unavailability of that day's quotation, the previous day's quotation was used [Figure 6-3(b)].

Remember, with a mutual fund, the value of its shares is important; but equally important is the number of shares you own. When a fund reinvests your dividends and capital gains, the share balance increases [Figure 6-1(g)]. Don't undervalue your fund by omitting these added shares.

If all these letters confuse you, take heart. At the bottom of the mutual fund quotation section is a short

---

Figure 6-3

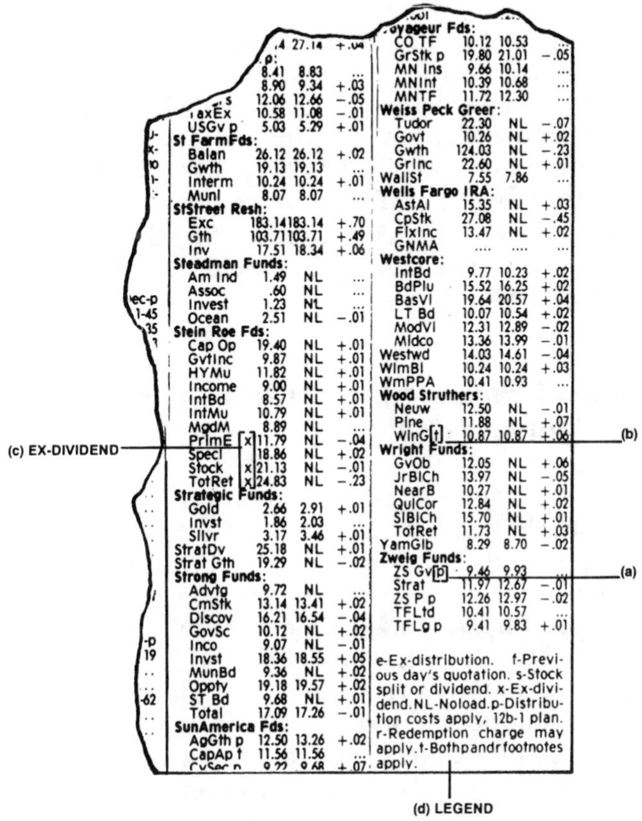

p:			
	8.41	8.83	...
	8.90	9.34	+.03
s	12.06	12.66	–.05
TaxEx	10.58	11.08	–.01
USGv p	5.03	5.29	+.01
St FarmFds:			
Balan	26.12	26.12	+.02
Gwth	19.13	19.13	...
Interm	10.24	10.24	+.01
Muni	8.07	8.07	...
StStreet Resh:			
Exc	183.14	183.14	+.70
Gth	103.71	103.71	+.49
Inv	17.51	18.34	+.06
Steadman Funds:			
Am Ind	1.49	NL	...
Assoc	.60	NL	...
Invest	1.23	NL	...
Ocean	2.51	NL	–.01
Stein Roe Fds:			
Cap Op	19.40	NL	+.01
GvtInc	9.87	NL	+.01
HYMu	11.82	NL	+.01
Income	9.00	NL	+.01
IntBd	8.57	NL	+.01
IntMu	10.79	NL	+.01
MgdM	8.89	NL	...
PrimE x	11.79	NL	–.04
Specl	18.86	NL	+.02
Stock x	21.13	NL	–.01
TotRet x	24.83	NL	–.23
Strategic Funds:			
Gold	2.66	2.91	+.01
Invst	1.86	2.03	...
Silvr	3.17	3.46	+.01
StratDv	25.18	NL	+.01
Strat Gth	19.29	NL	–.02
Strong Funds:			
Advtg	9.72	NL	...
CmStk	13.14	13.41	+.02
Discov	16.21	16.54	–.04
GovSc	10.12	NL	+.02
Inco	9.07	NL	–.01
Invst	18.36	18.55	+.05
MunBd	9.36	NL	+.02
Oppty	19.18	19.57	+.02
ST Bd	9.68	NL	+.01
Total	17.09	17.26	–.01
SunAmerica Fds:			
AgGth p	12.50	13.26	+.02
CapAp t	11.56	11.56	...
CvSec p	9.22	9.68	+.07

Voyageur Fds:			
CO TF	10.12	10.53	...
GrStk p	19.80	21.01	–.05
MN Ins	9.66	10.14	...
MNInt	10.39	10.68	...
MNTF	11.72	12.30	...
Weiss Peck Greer:			
Tudor	22.30	NL	–.07
Govt	10.26	NL	+.02
Gwth	124.03	NL	–.23
GrInc	22.60	NL	+.01
WallSt	7.55	7.86	...
Wells Fargo IRA:			
AstAl	15.35	NL	+.03
CpStk	27.08	NL	–.45
FlxInc	13.47	NL	+.02
GNMA	....	....	...
Westcore:			
IntBd	9.77	10.23	+.02
BdPlu	15.52	16.25	+.02
BasVl	19.64	20.57	+.04
LT Bd	10.07	10.54	+.02
ModVl	12.31	12.89	–.02
Midco	13.36	13.99	–.01
Westwd	14.03	14.61	–.04
WlmBl	10.24	10.24	+.03
WmPPA	10.41	10.93	...
Wood Struthers:			
Neuw	12.50	NL	–.01
Pine	11.88	NL	+.07
WinG t	10.87	10.87	+.06
Wright Funds:			
GvOb	12.05	NL	+.06
JrBlCh	13.97	NL	–.05
NearB	10.27	NL	+.01
QulCor	12.84	NL	+.02
SlBlCh	15.70	NL	+.01
TotRet	11.73	NL	+.03
YamGlb	8.29	8.70	–.02
Zweig Funds:			
ZS Gv p	9.46	9.93	...
Strat	11.97	12.67	–.01
ZS P p	12.26	12.97	–.02
TFLtd	10.41	10.57	...
TFLg p	9.41	9.83	+.01

e-Ex-distribution. f-Previous day's quotation. s-Stock split or dividend. x-Ex-dividend. NL-Noload. p-Distribution costs apply, 12b-1 plan. r-Redemption charge may apply. t-Both p and r footnotes apply.

legend explaining what they mean [Figure 6-3(d)]. Simply refer to the legend, and the mystery disappears.

Mutual fund numbers are important, but don't get so involved in them that you lose sight of their purpose. They are there to furnish data from which to make informed decisions. They tell how well your mutual fund is doing and whether it is keeping up with your goals. Numbers show whether your mutual fund is on target with your projections. Finally, they give an overall picture as to how the performance of your mutual fund compares with the market indexes—Standard & Poor's and the Dow. With this, you should be interested in answering the question...

How Do I Evaluate the Performance of My Mutual Fund?

Some months ago I received a report on a mutual fund I own that showed how my investment had grown over a 10-year period ending May 31, 1986. During that time the value of the fund had increased more than 600 percent. Apparently this raised some eyebrows among shareholders, so that the president of the fund began receiving letters questioning the accuracy of his figures. This prompted another message to shareholders explaining a very important feature of mutual fund investing—accumulation of shares. Although it has been mentioned in passing, it's a point so often overlooked or misunderstood by mutual fund clients that a brief review would be beneficial.

Mutual funds are required to distribute at least 90 percent of all investment profits. This is done through a dividend, or distribution. These distributions consist of (1) capital gains recognized by the fund from the sale of securities and (2) income paid to the fund from interest or dividends on the portfolio. At the end of the year, a summary of distributions is reported to you for income tax purposes. A copy is also sent to the Internal Revenue Service, which can then match your reported income with what the fund has reported paying. Whether to accept these mutual fund distributions in cash or to reinvest them in additional shares is your choice. But regardless of the choice—cash or reinvest—taxes are due on the distributions during the tax year they are declared. If you select to receive all distributions in cash, the number of fund shares you own remains constant. If on the other hand, you choose to reinvest these dividend distributions in additional shares, the number of shares you own increases and compounds. When measuring the performance of your fund, these distributions must be considered. Since the fund distributes most of the profits and income it earns, the quoted price of the fund could remain relatively unchanged, yet you continue to receive dividends.

For example, an examination of one shareholder's mutual fund statement in January 1986 showed he owned 7,538.873 shares [Figure 6-4(a)] with a net asset value of $16.29 [Figure 6-4(b)], a total value of $122,808.24. By the end of the year, the per share value was $18.36, up $2.07 [Figure 6-4(c)]. Not an overly impressive number, you say. However, during that year there was a total of $22,458.99 in dividends and gains, which he selected to reinvest in additional fund shares rather than accepting in cash [Figure 6-4(d)].

At year's end he had 1,274.12 more shares. He now owned 8,812.994 [Figure 6-4(e)] shares, valued at $18.36 each, for a total value of $161,806.57 [Figure 6-4(f)]. By reinvesting and compounding, he had increased the total value of his investment by $38,998.33, or 31.8 percent.

Keep in mind, these results are for the year 1986, which showed a market of generally rising stock prices. The purpose of this example is to illustrate that when measuring the performance of your mutual fund you

Figure 6-4

MOST ANY GROWTH-INCOME FUND, INC.
INDIVIDUAL RETIREMENT ACCOUNT

ACCOUNT NUMBER 1234567-0	SOCIAL SECURITY ON TAXPAYER IDENTIFICATION NO. (REQUIRED BY LAW) 444-444-444	SALES REPRESENTATIVE SERVICING YOUR ACCOUNT JOE SALESMAN	DEALER NO. BRANCH 123-4567

STATEMENT DATE
12/05/86

JOE E DOKES &
MARY Z DOKES   TEN COM
100 PLAZA
ANYTOWN, USA

ACCOUNT OPTION
DIV-R   CAP-R

INDIVIDUAL TRANSACTIONS FOR YEAR TO DATE

CONFIRM DATE	TRADE DATE	TRANSACTION DESCRIPTION		DOLLAR AMOUNT	PRICE PER SHARE	SHARE THIS TRANSACTION	TOTAL SHARES OWNED
		BEGINNING BALANCE					7,538.873 (a)
1/17	1/10	INCOME DIVIDEND	.18	1,357.00	16.290 (b)	83.303	7,622.176
1/17	1/10	CAPITAL GAIN	.86	6,483.43	16.290	398.001	8,020.177
4/18	4/11	INCOME DIVIDEND	.18	1,443.63	18.430 +$2.07	78.330	8,098.507 +$1274.12 SHS
7/18	7/11	INCOME DIVIDEND	.19	1,538.72	18.770	81.978	8,180.485
10/17	10/10	INCOME DIVIDEND	.19	1,554.29	18.640 (c)	83.385	8,263.870
12/12	12/05	CAPITAL GAIN	1.22	10,081.92	18.360	549.126	8,812.994 (e)

18.36 × 8812.994 = $161,806.57

**UNLESS THERE ARE SUBSEQUENT TRANSACTIONS IN YOUR ACCOUNT, THIS WILL BE YOUR FINAL STATEMENT FOR CALENDAR YEAR 1986.
PLEASE RETAIN FOR YOUR RECORDS.

YEAR TO DATE ACCOUNT SUMMARY

TOTAL DIVIDENDS AND OTHER DISTRIBUTIONS	LONG TERM CAPITAL GAINS DISTRIBUTIONS	CERTIFICATE SHARES	SHARES ON DEPOSIT IN ACCOUNT	TOTAL SHARES OWNED
22458.99 (d)	16665.35		8,812.996 (f)	8,812.96

This example is for illustrative purposes only and does not imply future results.

must consider (1) the number of shares owned, or accumulated, (2) any dividends you might select to receive in cash, and finally (3) the power of compounding.

Understand the performance of your mutual fund, and you will either be more comfortable with it or have reason to reconsider its investment value. Either way you win.

There usually comes a time when investors want, or need, to sell shares of common stock or mutual fund shares. Knowing how to sell is as important as knowing how to buy.

How Do I Sell My Mutual Fund Shares?

Common stock represents ownership in a corporation with shares listed for trading, usually on one of the major exchanges or the over-the-counter market. The shares are bought and sold by brokers registered to trade on those exchanges.

For example, if you wish to buy a stock trading on the New York Stock Exchange, you contact a broker who is a member of that exchange. Start by opening an account and agreeing on the price you will pay. Then have the broker buy the stock for you.

For a commission, your broker buys the stock, takes delivery, and pays for it. Your broker then has it reregistered in your name, delivers the stock, and collects from you. Although the mechanics can take several weeks, orders entered *at market* are executed immediately over the firm's *wire system*. So often you get the price within seconds.

When you decide to sell, the same process is followed. Once your broker is satisfied you hold the stock certificates in *good delivery*, the sale is made efficiently, and your transaction is reported almost immediately.

The sale or redemption of mutual fund shares, however, can be confusing. There are several ways mutual fund shares are redeemed.

Redemption is simple when you elect to have the fund hold the certificates in safekeeping with a custodian bank. With some funds this allows you to arrange redemption or transfer over the telephone. A call to the fund with your instructions is all it takes. You redeem your shares for the net asset value at the close of business on the day of the transaction.

If the broker through whom you purchased your shares is equipped to handle your order *by wire*, your shares are also redeemed at net asset value at the close of business. The broker collects the money and pays you. There is usually no charge for this service, but it's a good idea to establish this in advance.

You should also know whether your broker is equipped to liquidate by wire. If not, your fund shares are sold by mail. This could take several days, and the value of your shares could change appreciably before the fund receives your order.

I read a complaint about the broker of a shareholder who placed an order to sell on October 13, when the net asset value of his fund was $16.43. The order was mailed by the broker. It reached the fund and was executed on October 19, ""Black Monday," at a net asset value of $12.85.

This is, of course, an extreme example. It does illustrate, however, the importance of having your orders executed as efficiently as possible.

Once you decide to sell and are satisfied with the price, don't let your order remain in limbo. Avoid disappointment and misunderstanding. Know how to place your orders, and find out when they will be executed.

Of course, when you sell mutual fund shares, not all the money is necessarily yours to keep.

Who Shares My Profits or Losses?

Mutual funds enable you to invest when you have money available. They also allow you to reinvest capital gains and dividends so your money compounds. All these things, of course, occur at different times, and your shares are bought at different prices.

When you need money, the fund sells enough shares at the current net asset value and mails you a check. Net asset value is the current market value of a fund's shares minus any liabilities divided by the total number of shares outstanding.

Which shares you sell could make a big difference in the taxes you pay. Suppose you own 5,000 shares of ABC Fund. In 1978 you bought 3,000 shares at $10 a share. You added another 1,000 shares in 1988 at $20 a share, and in 1989 you bought the last 1,000 shares at $25 a share. Today the NAV of the fund shares is $20, and you ask the fund to send you $20,000. The fund sells 1,000 shares at $20, mails you a check, and reports the transaction to the Internal Revenue Service.

Because you did not specify which shares to sell, the IRS's *FIFO* (first in, first out) rule applies. In this case 1,000 of your January 1978 shares were sold, and your cost basis was $10,000. That gives you a profit of $10,000, which in the 28 percent tax bracket means a tax bill of $2,800.

Had you instructed the fund to sell the 1,000 shares you purchased for $25 a share, at a cost basis of $25,000, you would instead show a loss of $5,000. This loss could be applied against any gains you might have realized and could save you as much as $1,400 in taxes. If you had no gains in that particular year, $3,000 of the loss could be applied against ordinary income, and the remaining amount carried forward to the next year.

The IRS and the courts say shares must be identified by the date of purchase and price when the sell order is placed. The fund, on the other hand, shows on your confirmation statement only that shares were sold on a specific date at a specific price.

A spokesperson for the Capital Guardian Group, one of the nation's largest mutual fund managers, says it would be very difficult for them to identify specific shares sold. This seems to be a general practice in the industry.

Kathryn Morrison of the Investment Company Institute says that some fund groups might confirm in some way that your instructions were received. The burden of proof, however, is with you if you are questioned by the IRS.

Morrison offered some sound advice. Keep good records. This includes the fund's confirmation of your sell, the confirmation of the original buy, and your letter of instruction to the fund or your broker identifying the specific shares you wanted sold.

Will the IRS accept this? No one will say for sure, but most agree this method should work. Remember, once you begin identifying shares, you must keep accurate records so that the shares are not specified again for future sale.

Accurately determining the cost basis of your mutual fund shares requires some detail work, but it may save you money in taxes. This book is not a tax guide. IRS regulations change, and individual circumstances can alter the simplest rules. Always figure the tax consequence of any anticipated sale of mutual fund shares before you sell. Talk to a tax professional, and understand your tax liabilities. Once the transaction is completed, it's too late.

Chapter 7

Mutual Fund Costs: or, Why Isn't It Free?

> Nothing will dispel enthusiasm like
> a small admission fee.
> —*Ken Hubbard*

Whenever someone offers something for nothing, I am reminded of the slogan of Chilkoot Charlie's Saloon in Anchorage, Alaska, which promises, "We cheat the other guy and pass the savings on to you."

Everything has a price tag. Somebody pays. But it's hard to resist the promise of a "free lunch." After all, as Chilkoot Charlie says, it's the other guy who gets cheated.

Mutual funds are a business. Like any business they offer a product and service for which they receive a reasonable compensation. From that they pay the bills, meet the payroll, and have some profit left over for the owners. That's the American way. Nothing operates for free ... except the government. And we all pay for that!

If that makes sense, then you'll agree that there is no such thing as a pure no-load fund that costs you nothing. So step into my myth-destroying time tunnel and explore mutual fund costs.

How Do Fund Managers Get Paid?

A mutual fund is a corporation whose business is managing money and whose asset is a portfolio of marketable securities. A fund's success depends on convincing enough people to invest so the managers have enough money to buy stocks, bonds, and other securities. The managers are paid for their service. This cost is figured and reported as a percentage of the value of the fund. Management costs vary between less than 1/2 of 1 percent on the low side to 3 percent or more on the high side. Typically, as a fund becomes larger, the management costs become less as a percentage of the fund's value.

Management costs are an important factor in how well your fund performs. It's deducted before any dividends or gains are distributed to shareholders. For example, if you invest $10,000 into Fund A, with an annual management fee of 1/2 of 1 percent (about typical for a load fund, where there's a sales charge) your cost for management is $50. On the other hand, if you choose to invest in Fund B, with a management fee of 2 percent, your annual cost is $200.

Remember, the management costs are paid each year, regardless of the performance of the fund. Don't confuse this management cost with the sales charge paid to the broker or dealer who sells the fund and services your account. A sales charge is generally paid only once on your original investment. If in several years your original $10,000 investment has grown to $20,000, the management cost for that year would be $100 for Fund A and $400 for Fund B. Let's compare two funds, each with a reasonable 15 percent average compound total return over a five-year period, and see how the management fee becomes significant.

Year	Value of Shares	Fund A (1/2 of 1%)	Fund B (2%)
1	10,000	50	200
2	11,000	55	220
3	15,000	75	300
4	17,000	85	340
5	20,000	100	400
		$385	$1,460

Over five years you'd have paid the manager of Fund B a total of $1,460, or 14.6 percent of your original investment. To Fund A you'd have paid only $365, or 3.7 percent of your original $10,000 investment.

Although no investment should be made or rejected only on the basis of cost, it should be considered. The information on management costs is found in the condensed financial information of the prospectus or in the fund's annual report. It is generally described as the "ratio of expense to average net assets" and is shown for past years as well as the current year.

The prospectus also provides information on the fund's management—who they are, their experience, other managed assets, agreements with the fund, and so on. When you invest in a fund, you're buying management. The fund's record shows how well or how poorly the fund's past management has done. It's your responsibility to investigate the consistency and reliability of management. Decide whether that record has a reasonable chance to continue. Does the management and its cost merit your investment confidence?

Ideally your fund's annual management costs should not exceed 1/2 of 1 percent of assets. This means that on a fund balance of $10,000, you'd pay only $50 that year to have your investment professionally managed. That would make your costs among the lowest, compared with an average of about 1.25 percent.

Generally, the larger the fund, the smaller the percentage should be. For example, for a small fund with $100 million in assets, a 1/2 of 1 percent management cost generates $500,000. This may sound like a lot of money, but with today's cost of operation, there would be little left for research portfolio managers and staff, not to mention a reasonable profit for the fund. If this same fund managed $1 billion, and other managed assets increased this to $10 billion or more, that same 1/2 of 1 percent management cost brings more than $50 million to the fund annually. With this the fund can hire and offer to shareholders top analysts, portfolio managers, customer services, and more.

Management costs are an annual expense. In a special 1986 edition of *Money* magazine, from 154 major funds surveyed, the management fee ranged from a high of 3.47 percent annually (a no-load fund) to a low of .44 percent (a load fund). Remember, all cost information is in the prospectus if you look for it. Funds with high management costs seldom make an issue of telling you about it, so it's up to you to find it.

Fees and costs are part of doing business. Management is entitled to reasonable compensation for services, and stockholders are entitled to reasonable profit on investment. Don't be misled into thinking you're getting your service free. Management is a cost of all mutual funds. Know where to look for that cost in the prospectus. Make sure the results merit the cost.

The next cost is the acquisition cost, sales charge, or load. What if one mutual fund charges a load and another claims no-load?

Why Invest in a Load Fund When I Can Have a No-Load?

When you select a mutual fund, be sure your choice is based on your objective, the fund's risk, and the consistency of the fund's management performance. There are other factors, but if you and the fund share the same goals and it has a good record of meeting those goals, that's a good reason to own it.

Americans like a bargain. Why pay for a service you can get free? Mutual fund investors are no exception. Why pay a load, a front-end sales charge, when you can buy a no-load fund instead? It's a reasonable question that deserves consideration.

In a medical emergency the first concern is to get the best care possible. Paying for it comes later. This is true with most important decisions. What's best—not how much does it cost—is the essential question.

With investing, however, the cost of service often overshadows the quality of service. Mutual fund fees can add to this confusion.

A fee that has become a point of discussion is the load, or acquisition cost. Pay a fee when you buy a mutual fund, and it's a load. The load can be as much as 8.5 percent of the offering price, or less than 1 percent. It's based on how much you invest. The load is easily found and explained in the prospectus.

If a fund decides to charge fees when you sell, or to add a fee each year for the expense of running the fund, it could be called a no-load. A no-load with charges? That's right, look in the prospectus.

Fees charged by many funds fall under Rule 12b-1 of the Investment Company Act of 1940. This allows certain marketing expenses to be charged to the fund's assets. These expenses, paid by the fund but charged to you (my words, not theirs), vary depending upon how much new money is being added to the fund.

As required, these funds refer you to the prospectus for details. The prospectus generally promises no sales charge when you buy. But there may be a deferred sales charge when you sell.

If imposed, the deferred sales charge is deducted from your redemption proceeds and retained by the fund.

That means this particular no-load fund just got a sales charge.

Finally the prospectus may explain why there is no front-end sales charge and why this fund is a no-load fund. Generally that explanation tells how it allows them to bear some of the costs of selling its shares under a distribution plan adopted pursuant to Rule 12b-1. That means the load is hidden under another name.

If all this sounds confusing, it is. Some no-load funds can not only charge a withdrawal fee but can also charge an additional fee of up to 1.25 percent annually of the fund's average daily net assets. Add this to a management fee that could be higher than some similar load funds, and you see the hidden charges the average bargain-hunting investor could encounter.

My purpose is not to discourage investing in no-load funds. Some have excellent investment records and offer a knowledgeable investor an inexpensive way to benefit from the professional management of mutual funds. If you are such a person, looking for a true no-load fund, look beyond the no-load promise and ask yourself...

When Is a No-Load Not a No-Load?

Remember, the sales charge is a fee paid to brokers for marketing the fund's shares and servicing the account in future years.

In 1980 the SEC Rule 12b-1 permitted a special deduction from the fund's assets for commissions, advertising, and marketing. This is in addition to, and sometimes larger than, the management fee and isn't considered a load as far as the 8.5 percent limit is concerned.

A *contingent deferred sales charge* is another way to collect commissions. These fees are deducted if you redeem your shares before a specified time. For example, a fund might charge a contingent deferred charge of 5 percent during the first year, 4 percent the second year, 3 percent the third, and lesser percentages until the seventh year, when there is no charge.

Other funds may charge a *redemption fee* rather than an up-front charge. A straight redemption fee differs from the contingent deferred sales charge in that it's charged against the total value of your shares. That includes not only your original investment but also any profits you may have earned during that time.

To further complicate sales costs, there are mutual fund groups that offer their funds either way—pay now or pay later. For example, *Changing Times*, in a special February 1989 report on mutual fund loads versus no-loads, shows one major group that offers two versions of their 22 different funds.

Their Class A fund charges the traditional front-end load, up to a maximum of 6.5 percent. The Class B fund charges no front-end load but rather collects a redemption fee of up to 4 percent plus an annual 12b-1 fee of up to 1 percent.

Other funds utilize the 12b-1 charges but allow those charges to fall substantially after the fifth or sixth year. In such cases it's wise to be certain you won't need to withdraw your funds within the first year or two.

Other traditional "no-load" funds impose a "low load" of 3 percent or less on their more popular funds. They justify this as advertising costs. After all, since there are no brokers to promote it, the fund must advertise in order to bring in new capital. Regardless of the reason, you pay the cost.

The 12b-1 fee has created controversy since its inception. What makes 12b-1 a bitter pill for many investors is that it can be assessed forever, creating effectively a no-limit sales charge. To add insult to injury, they can call it a no-load fund. As investors become more aware of 12b-1 fees, their protests increase.

Like any controversy, there are two sides to the 12b-1 question. On the plus side, many major load mutual funds that select to use 12b-1 reduce their initial sales charge. In some cases the 8.5 percent maximum load has been reduced to 5.75 percent or less. Volume discounts further reduce charges. This allows you to buy the fund at a lower initial cost and have more invested dollars at work immediately. Each year, however, a 12b-1 fee is deducted from your fund's net asset value and shared with the brokers who sold you the fund. This is not intended as a bonus for brokers. It is paid by the fund only to brokers who continue to service your account.

But what if you get no service and still pay 12b-1 fees? That's the rub.

The National Association of Securities Dealers (NASD) and the Securities and Exchange Commission are working on a plan to give mutual fund investors a break from unreasonable 12b-1 fees.

A. John Taylor, vice president of the NASD, is reported to be working on a plan whereby a shareholder would have to pay no more through 12b-1 charges than about what the maximum front-end load would be. The plan would effectively lower initial charges regardless of what they are called—front loads, rear loads, or 12b-1 fees. It would, however, allow the fund to levy a reasonable and limited annual fee for servicing. Funds that utilize the 12b-1 fee could no longer be called no-load under the proposed plan. Once the plan is finalized, it goes to the NASD membership for a vote and finally to the SEC for approval.

It is also reported that the SEC is working on its own plan to overhaul the 12b-1 fees. At this writing no details are known.

There is no doubt that as mutual fund shareholders increase in number and demand more in service, the funds must tap their assets to pay these costs. Time will tell if 12b-1 fees will continue to be that source.

As always, when changes come they must be explained in the fund's prospectus. Don't be misled by general reportings of 12b-1 changes. They may continue to offer funds some flexibility as to their use. Read the fund's prospectus to know your costs. And don't be afraid to ask questions.

How do you unscramble all these costs, charges, and loads? Read the prospectus. Short of that, a reasonable understanding of the mutual fund page in most major newspapers gives a general idea of *how* the fund charges—but not *how much* it charges. Be ready for a lot of abbreviations and several trips to the footnotes. Here are a few examples that will help with the task.

NL – No front-end sales charge.

p – These funds charge an annual 12b-1 fee. A fund can be listed NL and still charge this fee. The prospectus tells how much.

r – Watch redemption charges. These charges can be permanent, temporary, or declining. These can also pass as NL. The prospectus is your only protection.

p and r – These funds charge both a 12b-1 fee and a redemption fee. Pay special attention to these charges. They can be confusing and expensive.

These aren't all the newspaper symbols; however, they offer a good sampling of costs and descriptions. Although costs are not the major reason for investing in a mutual fund, the ICI found they do influence 28 percent of the investors who buy shares direct from the fund. In the same investor survey it was found that of the 44 percent who bought a fund on the recommendation of a sales representative, only 8 percent bought because of lower costs (Appendix 4).

There are other fees that may be uncovered in a fund's prospectus. For example, start-up fees, transfer agency fees, and account maintenance fees can all be charged in addition to the management fee. These added fees and methods of charging commissions make it more important than ever to read and understand the fund's prospectus. In addition, make sure the many services provided free through a conventional load fund aren't eliminated in a no-load fund.

Those modest charges add up to a lot more over the long haul than a simple up-front load. Don't confuse no-load with no-cost.

Chapter 8

AFTER THE CRASH: OR, WHERE DO I GO NOW?

Those who have never made a mistake
work for those who have dared to.
—*Leon Sokolsky*

Although there is strong justification for long-term investing, even the staunchest buckled under the stock market crash of October 1987. It didn't take a lot of study to see investor confidence eroding.

The October 1987 market meltdown led some investors to question the logic of long-term investing. After all, a market decline of almost 20 percent in one day is a good argument for short-term investing and market timing.

Wouldn't it be more profitable to anticipate market tops and withdraw before they occur? Yes, but no one has yet devised a system to accurately predict when the market will top or hit bottom. If such a crystal ball existed, investors could prudently withdraw principal and profits from the market and reinvest in the safety and higher yields of bonds or other debt instruments. When the market bottomed, they could return to equities.

Unfortunately, this seldom happens, but many refuse to recognize it. They cling to the hope that somewhere there is a Santa Claus.

Look at the historical case for long-term investing versus market timing.

Kenneth Janke, president of the NAIC, an organization of individual investors and investment clubs, recently pointed out that a market timer has to be right 80 percent of the time to match the performance of a long-term investor.

Although you might quibble with Janke's estimate, a strong case for a buy-and-hold strategy can be made by looking at the closing prices for the Dow Jones Industrial Average since 1946. The Dow has closed up in 28 of those 42 years. In order to have profited from market timing, you would have had to have been right 67 percent of the time just to match the buy-and-hold strategy. Since bull market gains are historically greater than bear market losses, Janke's 80 percent estimate could be correct.

That alone is a good argument for long-term investing. Add to it the cost and tax liabilities of in-and-out trading, and you have a convincing argument for even the staunchest trader.

If there is a profit, taxes can claim up to 33 percent of that. It means you are taking the risk and sharing the profits with your broker and the Internal Revenue Service. This does not mean it cannot be done effectively. The message is that investing should be a long-range plan of putting money to work now to benefit you later. How your investments perform over short periods is not as important as how much is there when you need it.

There are few guarantees, so it's important to keep the odds on your side when planning. But even with logic and evidence of rewards in long-term investing, there remains a nagging doubt.

In Light of the 1987 Stock Market Crash, Does It Still Make Sense to Own Mutual Funds?

According to a study reported by the *Wall Street Journal*, during the first quarter of 1988 money flowed out of stock funds sold by brokers. The Investment Company Institute pointed out, however, that money continued to seep slowly into direct-market (no-load) funds.

The confidence gap appeared to be more in the salesperson who recommended the fund rather than the performance of the fund itself. John Markese, research director for the American Association of Individual Investors, a Chicago-based nonprofit group, suggested the salesperson just wasn't there when needed.

The Wall Street Journal discovered that investors were pressing for more reliable guidance. One mutual fund offered a work sheet to help investors set goals. There was an immediate and "unprecedented" 40,000 replies. Another mutual fund group received several thousand requests from their advertisement for a free brochure on how to be your own portfolio manager.

The conclusion from this study appears to be that, in the euphoria of a runaway bull market, many investors were sold mutual funds with expectations of unrealistic gains. Unfortunately, equal time was not given to the risks. When a market correction eventually came, the salesperson who painted this rosy picture was nowhere to be found.

How Bad Was the Drop?

Changing Times magazine did a special report in February 1988 on mutual funds. The stock market topped out August 25, 1987. By December 1, the Dow Jones Industrial Average had fallen 32 percent.

How did our five basic groups of mutual funds compare?

The aggressive growth funds and sector funds lost about the same, 32 percent. Growth and income funds did slightly better, with a minus 27 percent. Balanced funds, because they owned both stocks and bonds, lost 17 percent. Income funds, holding mostly bonds and a few equities, suffered least with a 10 percent loss.

Keep in mind, however, that these figures reflect the time from when the market peaked until just after the crash, not a very representative picture of overall long-term performance.

Just days after the market crash, *The Wall Street Journal* released a study of how the country's biggest and best-known stock funds fared. These nine largest funds manage assets of almost $30 billion. All have over $1 billion in assets, with an average of $3.3 billion.

One week after the crash, October 26, 1987, these giant funds had lost an average of 27.7 percent in assets. This compares favorably with the loss of 29.1 percent in the Standard & Poor's 500 Index. Four of these funds were growth funds, four growth and income funds, and one a global fund. The funds that favored growth over income were hardest hit.

An interesting point, however, is that for the entire year—January 1, 1987, through October 26, 1987—the funds were off only an average of 4.9 percent, with two of the group showing fractional gains. The largest loss in any one fund for that period was 10.5 percent.

Johnson's Charts, an independent research firm that follows almost 1300 different mutual funds, reported for the period ending December 31, 1987, that the *average* of their fund categories showed minor gains in total return. The report also indicated that for the period ending December 31, 1988, one year after the market crash, the average of all fund categories posted significant gains.

What Does the Outcome of the 1987 Crash Mean?

Those investors who did their homework and put confidence in the professional management of proven mutual funds that met their needs and risk tolerance emerged with the fewest scars from the market crash. Those who abandoned long-term goals or were sold on short-term stardom generally suffered.

Broad-sweeping generalities, regardless of their wisdom, seldom offer much guidance to chart a financial future. So let's wrap it all up with 10 solid rules you can hold on to.

Chapter 9

PUTTING IT ALL TOGETHER: OR, WHY NOT WRAP IT UP IN 10 EASY RULES?

Eternal Vigilance Is the Price of Safety.
—*Wall Street axiom*

Henry Ford viewed money quite simply. "Money," said Ford, "is like an arm or a leg—use it or lose it." In investing it's a bit more complicated. Money must be used *prudently* or, as Ford warns, it's lost.

The stock market has become a market of professionals, as the tremendous daily trading volume testifies. At one time 10 million shares exchanged in a single day was active. Today over-100-million-share days are routine.

But the individual investor is still in the market. He must be to share in the economy. Today more investors are participating through the purchase of mutual fund shares, leaving the day-to-day decision making to the professionals. Yet the mere fact that mutual funds are popular, with long records of proven investment results, does not guarantee that all mutual funds are good investments. The proper fund, like the proper stock, must be carefully selected and matched to your investment goals. To summarize and bind it in a neat little package for everyday use, here are 10 easy rules to guide you *before* you invest and help you follow your progress *after* you invest.

Rule 1: Know Your Fund's Manager. (Chapter 2) Study the performance of the management group that manages not only your fund but also others within that family of funds. Compare their results with other management groups. Money management is what you are buying. Make sure you buy wisely.

Rule 2: Know Your Fund's Research and Analysts. Ask about the fund's research and research analysts—how many, their qualifications, techniques of research, sources of research material, and the like. The quality of research determines investment results. Research analysts supply the raw material for investment decisions.

Rule 3: Read Financial Publications. (Chapter 3) The business page of your daily newspaper, financial magazines, and services such as Lipper, Wiesenberger, and Johnson offer excellent information on mutual funds. Understand fund performance and how it's calculated for similar funds with your investment objective.

Rule 4: Read Your Prospectus. (Chapter 3) The prospectus is the story of your mutual fund. It includes such vital information as the fund's objectives, management, fees, expenses, and more. The prospectus is so important that the fund is legally required to give it to you before accepting your investment. So read and understand the prospectus.

Rule 5: Diversify. (Chapters 1, 2, 3) Although a mutual fund offers immediate diversification by investing in many different corporations, it is well to consider diversification among and within mutual fund groups. By carefully selecting a family of funds, diversification can generally be done simply and inexpensively both now and in the future. By diversifying assets you reduce risk.

Rule 6: Keep Records. (Chapter 6) Good records are necessary not only for tax purposes but also to let you know how your investment is progressing. Most mutual funds furnish excellent records, notifying you whenever a transaction takes place in your account—additional deposits or withdrawals, reinvestment of dividends, capital gains, and the like. It's important that you read, understand, and keep these records.

Rule 7: Monitor Investment Results. (Chapter 6) In a mutual fund the fund managers monitor their investments on a full-time basis. This relieves you of some responsibility. That does not suggest that you buy shares of a mutual fund, forget them, and come back years later expecting to be rich. Don't be overly concerned by short-term fluctuations, but when your quarterly statements and reports arrive, study them carefully and keep track of your investment.

Rule 8: Invest Regularly. (Chapter 4) One of the best ways to make your money work for you, regardless of market conditions, is dollar cost averaging—investing equal amounts at regular intervals. Although not a guarantee of profit, dollar cost averaging does take the worry out of when to invest. It's a rational and systematic investment strategy.

Rule 9: Be Flexible. (Chapters 1, 4) No investment is forever. As your needs change, so should your investments. If you prepare for those future investment needs by selecting the proper family of funds, when the need for change arrives, it can be made simply and inexpensively. Anticipate change and plan for it. Change is one thing you can count on.

Rule 10: Use Your Broker. (Chapter 1) Today there are almost 2,000 different mutual funds offering shares to the public. A costly mistake is to consider your broker as your order taker. I equally discourage blindly accepting any mutual fund he offers. Your broker should be a registered investment specialist and as such have a wealth of information available to help you select the mutual fund best suited to your investment objective. After you have invested, he should continue to work with you, helping monitor your fund, offering assistance and advice. Use his services selectively.

Mutual funds are an excellent way to use your money and have it work for you. But just as important as using it is using it wisely.

This book does not, nor is it intended to, answer all mutual fund questions. Hopefully, it has stimulated your interest in mutual funds so that you want to consider them as another investment option. Of course, you can always visit your local bookstore for another, more advanced mutual fund text. Then you will be more informed. But who wants to be an encyclopedia of mutual fund data? All the guidelines you need for successful mutual fund investing are within these pages. Investing, like swimming, is a participation event. Learning is important, but until you get wet you aren't a swimmer; and until you invest, you aren't an investor.

Although my suggestions are not written in stone, they represent the accumulation of almost 25 years of professional investing experience. Consider them, select several mutual funds, and play with the puzzle. Set your goals and follow the bouncing ball over the 10 easy rules. Good fortune and good investing!

Glossary of Mutual Fund Terms

Annual Report—The formal financial statement issued yearly by a corporation or mutual fund. It shows the financial status of the company, how well the company progressed during the business year, and other information of value and interest to shareholders.

Asked (or Offering) Price—The price at which a mutual fund's shares can be purchased. The asked (or offering) price is the current net asset value plus any sales charge.

Automatic Reinvestment—An option available to mutual fund shareholders that allows dividends and capital gains to be automatically put back into the fund to buy new shares and increase holdings.

Bid (or Redemption) Price—(As seen in some mutual fund newspaper listings.) The price at which a mutual fund's shares are redeemed (bought back) by the fund. The bid or redumption price usually equals the current net asset value.

Broker—An agent who handles the public's orders to buy and sell securities, commodities, or other property. For this service a commission is charged.

Capital Gains Distributions—Payment to shareholders of a mutual fund of gains on the sale of the fund's securities. These are generally paid once a year.

Capital Growth—An increase in the market value of a mutual fund's securities, as reflected in the net asset value of fund shares.

Compound Interest—Interest computed on principal plus interest accrued during a previous period or periods. Interest can be computed monthly, quarterly, semiannually or annually for compounding.

Custodian—The organization (usually a bank) that keeps custody of securities and other assets of a mutual fund.

Dividend—Paid to owners of common stock, preferred stock, or mutual funds at the discretion of the board of directors. Dividends are paid from the company's present or past earnings. Many growth companies pay little or no dividend, in order to use these earnings for future development and company growth.

Diversification—Spreading investments among a variety of different securities to reduce the risk.

Dollar Cost Averaging—Buying securities or mutual fund shares at regular intervals with a fixed dollar amount—buying a given amount of money's worth, and not a specific number, or shares.

Exchange Privilege—Allows mutual fund shareholders to transfer their investment from one fund to another within the same fund family. Usually funds let investors use the exchange privilege several times a year for a low, or no, fee per exchange.

Government Bonds—Obligations of the U.S. govermemt. regarded as the highest-grade issues in existance.

Income Dividends—Payments made to shareholders of dividends, interest, and short-term capital gains earned on the fund's investments after operating expenses have been deducted.

Institutional Investor—An organization whose primary purpose is to invest its own assets or those held in trust by it for others. This includes pension funds, investment companies, insurance companies, universities, and banks.

Investment Company—A company or trust that uses its capital to invest in other companies. There are two principal types: the closed-end and the open-end, or mutual fund. Shares in the closed-end investment companies, some of which are listed on the New York Stock Exchange, are readily transferable in the open market and are bought and sold like other shares. Capitalization of these companies remains the same unless action is taken to change. Open-end funds are so called because their capitalization isn't fixed; they issue more shares as people want them.

Investment Counsel—One whose principal business consists of acting as investment adviser. A substantial part of an investment counsel's business consists of rendering supervisory services.

Investment Objective—The goal (e.g., growth or income) that an investor or mutual fund pursues.

Management Fee—The fee paid to an investment manager. This is most frequently associated with a mutual fund, although it applies to any investment manager. For a mutual fund, the fee generally averages about 1/2 of 1 percent of the total net assets per year. This amounts to about $5 for every $1000 of assets.

Mutual Fund—An open-end investment company. It offers new shares to the public continuously and is required by law to redeem outstanding shares on demand.

Net Asset value—A term usually used in connection with investment companies meaning *true value per share*. It is common practice for an investment company to compute its assets daily, or even twice daily, by totalling the market value of all securities owned. All liabilities are deducted, and the balance is divided by the number of shares outstanding. The resulting figure is the net asset value.

Open-End Investment Company—The statutory terminology for a mutual fund, indicating that it stands ready to redeem (buy back) its shares on demand.

Portfolio—Securities owned by an individual or institution. A portfolio may contain bonds, preferred stocks, and common stocks of various types of enterprises.

Prospectus—The legal document that offers a mutual fund or new issue of securities to the public. It is required under the Securities Act of 1933.

Redemption Price—The amount per share that mutual fund shareholders receive when they liquidate their shares (also knows as the *bid price*).

Reinvestment Privilege—A service provided by most mutual funds for the automatic reinvestment of shareholder dividends and capital gains distributions into additional shares.

Sales Charge—The cost to purchase shares in many mutual funds. Typically the charge ranges from 4 to 8.5 percent of the initial investment. The charge is added to the net asset value when determining the offering price.

Speculation—The employment of funds by individuals who take risks. Safety of principal is a secondary factor.

Total Return—The price gain plus reinvested dividends and capital gains distribution of a mutual fund. It is generally expressed as a percentage of the value of the fund.

Transfer Agent—The organization employed by a mutual fund to prepare and maintain records relating to the accounts of its shareholders.

12b-1 Fee—Fee charged by some funds and named after the 1980 Securities and Exchange Commission rule that permits them. Such fees pay for distribution costs such as advertising or for commissions paid to brokers. The fund's prospectus details 12b-1 charges if applicable.

Unsecured Notes—IOUs issued by a company promising to repay borrowed principal at a specified date, and interest on the principal until fully repaid. It is backed by no collateral but is issued on the company's good name and promise to pay.

Withdrawal Plan—A way shareholders receive payments from their mutual fund investments at regular intervals. Generally these payments are drawn from the fund's dividends and capital gains distributions, if any, and from principal as needed.

Yield—Often referred to as *return* on your investment, yield is the dividend or interest paid on a stock or bond expressed as a percentage of the offering price. For example, if you place $100 in an investment that has paid $5 in income for the preceding 12 months, your expected yield is 5 percent.

APPENDICES

Appendix 1
More Funds from Which to Choose

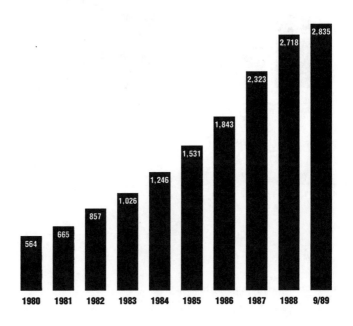

Source: Investment Company Institute

Appendix 2
How Investments in Funds Have Changed
(percentage distribution of assets)

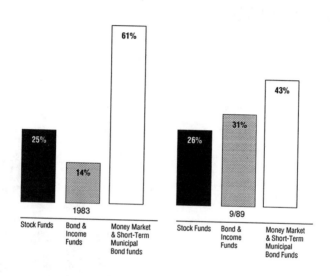

Source: Investment Company Institute

Appendix 3
What Diversification Means for Stock Mutual Funds
1938

If the portfolios of 60 of the largest stock mutual
funds were combined, the resulting total
would be invested as indicated
in the following industries

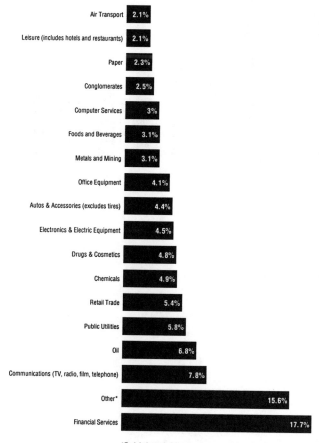

Industry	Percentage
Air Transport	2.1%
Leisure (includes hotels and restaurants)	2.1%
Paper	2.3%
Conglomerates	2.5%
Computer Services	3%
Foods and Beverages	3.1%
Metals and Mining	3.1%
Office Equipment	4.1%
Autos & Accessories (excludes tires)	4.4%
Electronics & Electric Equipment	4.5%
Drugs & Cosmetics	4.8%
Chemicals	4.9%
Retail Trade	5.4%
Public Utilities	5.8%
Oil	6.8%
Communications (TV, radio, film, telephone)	7.8%
Other*	15.6%
Financial Services	17.7%

*Each industry in this category represents less than 2% of total.

Source: Investment Company Institute

Appendix 4
How Investors Choose Among Different Funds
(percent of respondents to a 1986 ICI survey)

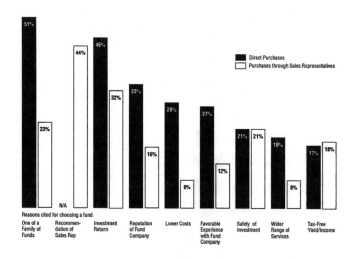

Source: Investment Company Institute

Appendix 5
Dollars Invested in All Types of Mutual Funds
(assets in billions)

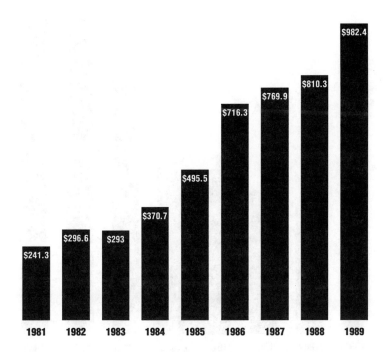

Source: Investment Company Institute

Appendix 6
Number of Shareholder Accounts in Mutual Funds
(millions)

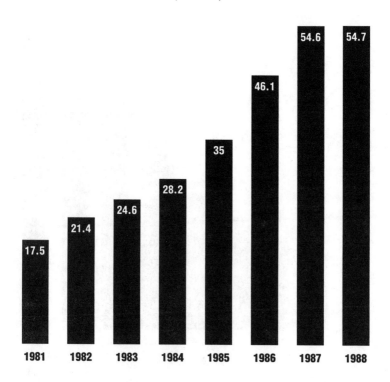

Source: Investment Company Institute

INDEX

About the Author

Robert Upton has almost twenty five years of investment experience, plus a long list of publications to his credit, including a syndicated investment column called *Financial Focus*.

He received his Bachelor's degree from the University of St. Mary's in San Antonio, Texas, and completed his graduate work at Pepperdine University. His Doctorate is from Kennedy-Western University. He is registered with the New York Stock Exchange and the National Association of Security Dealers, having served both as an investment broker and a manager of member firms.

Robert Upton's columns appear in more than 800 newspapers nationwide. His television program, *Robert Upton's Financial Focus*, airs weekly. He lectures professionally as a member of The International Platform Association and is a Louisiana College faculty member.

He has also been recognized in *Who's Who in the South*, the *International Who's Who of Intellectuals*, and *Who's Who in Finance and Industry*. He is a professional member of The National Writers Club.

**Additional Quick Reference Titles
Available from Probus Publishing:**

Financial Statement Analysis: The Basics & Beyond, Rose Marie L. Bukics, $12.95

Wall Street Words: The Basics & Beyond, Richard J. Maturi, $12.95